The Castle Spectre

M.G. Lewis

Copyright Notice

The text in this book has been downloaded from the internet and has been extensively edited and typeset.

Copyright © 2006 Objective Systems Pty Ltd ACN 085 119 953

CONTENTS

TO THE READER	V
ACT I	1
ACT II	25
ACT III	50
ACT IV	71
ACT V	93
EPILOGUE	117

First performed at the Theatre Royal, Drury-Lane, on Thursday, December 14, 1797.

II

Io me n'andro colla barchetta mia,
Quanto l'acqua comporta un picciol legno;
E ciò, ch'io penso colla fantasia,
Di piacere ad ognuno è il mio disegno:
Ben so, che spesso, come gia Morgante,
Lasciato ho forse troppo andar la mazza;
Ma dove fia poi judice bastante,
Materia c'è da camera, e da piazza.

– PULCI.

III

Spoken by Mr. Wroughton.

Far from the haunts of men, of vice the foe,
The moonstruck child of genius and of woe,
Versed in each magic spell, and dear to fame,
A fair enchantress dwells, Romance her name.
She loathes the sun, or blazing taper's light:
The moonbeam'd landscape and tempestuous night
Alone she loves; and oft, with glimmering lamp,
Near graves new-open'd, or 'midst dungeons damp,
Drear forests, ruin'd aisles, and haunted towers,
Forlorn she roves, and raves away the hours!
Anon, when storms howl loud and lash the deep,
Desperate she climbs the sea-rock's beetling steep;
There wildly strikes her harp's fantastic strings,
Tells to the moon how grief her bosom wrings,
And while her strange song chaunts fictitious ills,
In wounded hearts Oblivion's balm distills.
A youth, who yet has lived enough to know
That life has thorns, and taste the cup of woe,
As late near Conway's time-bowed towers he stray'd,
Invok'd this bright enthusiast's magic aid.
His prayer was heard. With arms and bosom bare,
Eyes flashing fire, loose robes, and streaming hair,
Her heart all anguish, and her soul all flame,
Swift as her thoughts, the lovely maniac came!
High heav'd her breasts, which struggling passions rent,
As prest to give some fear-fraught mystery vent:
And oft, with anxious glance and alter'd face,
Trembling with terror, she relaxed her pace,
And stopt! and listened! – Then with hurried tread
Onwards again she rush'd, yet backwards bent her head,

IV

As if from murderous swords or following fiends she fled!
Soon as near Conway's walls her footsteps drew,
She bade the youth their ancient state renew:
Eager he sped the fallen towers to rear:
'Twas done, and fancy bore the fabric here.
Next choosing from great Shakspeare's comic school,
The gossip crone, gross friar, and gibing fool—
These, with a virgin fair and lover brave,
To our young author's care the enchantress gave;
But charged him, ere he bless'd the brave and fair,
To lay th'exulting villain's bosom bare,
And by the torments of his conscience show,
That prosperous vice is but triumphant woe!
The pleasing task, congenial to his soul,
Oft from his own sad thoughts our author stole:
Blest be his labours, if with like success
They soothe their sorrows whom I now address.
Beneath this dome, should some afflicted breast
Mourn slighted talents, or desert opprest,
False friendship, hopeless love, or faith betray'd;
Our author will esteem each toil o'er-paid,
If, while his muse exerts her livelier vein,
Or tells imagined woes in plaintive strain,
Her flights and fancies make one smile appear
On the pale cheek, where trickled late a tear;
Or if her fabled sorrows steal one groan,
Which else her hearers would have given their own.

TO THE READER

Many erroneous assertions have been made respecting this Drama; some that the language was originally extremely licentious; others, that the sentiments were violently democratic; and others again, that if Mr. Sheridan had not advised me to content myself with a single Spectre, I meant to have exhibited a whole regiment of Ghosts. To disprove these reports I have deviated from the usual mode of publishing Plays, as performed, and have printed mine almost verbatim, as originally written. Whether it merited the above accusations, the reader has now had an opportunity of judging for himself. I must just mention that the last line of the Piece is altered, and that in the Second Scene of the Fifth Act, The Friar was made to stick in the doorway, whereas he now makes his exit without difficulty.

Other charges, however, have been brought against me on better grounds, and I must request the reader's patience while I say a few words respecting them. To originality of character I make no pretence. Persecuted heroines and conscience-stung villains certainly have made their courtesies and bows to a British audience long before the appearance of 'The Castle Spectre'; the Friar and Alice are copies, but very faint ones, from Juliet's Nurse, and Sheridan's Father Paul, and Percy is a mighty pretty-behaved young gentleman with nearly no character at all. I shall not so readily give up my claim to novelty, when I mention my misanthropic Negro. He has been compared to Zanga; but Young's Hero differs widely from what I meant in Hassan. Zanga's hatred is confined to one object; to destroy the happiness of that object is his sole aim, and his vengeance is no sooner accomplished, than he repents its gratification. Hassan is a man of violent passions, and warm feelings, whose bosom is filled with the milk of human kindness, but that milk is soured by despair; whose nature was susceptible of the tenderest affections, but who feels that all the chains of his affections are broken for ever. He has lost every thing, even hope; he has no single object against which he can direct his vengeance, and he directs it at large against mankind. He hates all the world, hates even himself; for he feels that in the world there is no one that loves him

> 'Lorsque l'on peut souffrir, sure que ses douleurs
> 'D'aucun mortel ne font jamais couler les pleurs,
> 'On se desinteresse à la fin de soi-même;
> 'On cesse de s'aimer, si quelqu'un ne nous aime!'

But though Hassan's heart is changed by disappointment and misfortune, that heart once was feeling and kind; nor could he hate with such inveteracy, if he had not loved with extreme affection. In my opinion this character is not Zanga's; but this I must leave to the public decision. I may, however, boldly, and without vanity, assert, that Motley is quite new to the Stage. In other plays the Fool has always been a sharp knave, quick in repartee, and full of whim, fancy, and entertainment; whereas my Fool (but I own I did not mean to make him so) is a dull, flat, good sort of plain matter of fact fellow, as in the course of the performance Mr. Bannister discovered to his great sorrow.

That Osmond is attended by Negroes is an anachronism, I allow; but from the great applause which Mr. Dowton constantly received in Hassan (a character which he played extremely well), I am inclined to think that the audience was not greatly offended at the impropriety. For my own part, I by no means repent the introduction of my Africans: I thought it would give a pleasing variety to the characters and dresses, if I made my servants black; and could I have produced the same effect by making my heroine blue, blue I should have made her.

In the Friar's defence, when he most ungallantly leaves Angela in the cavern to shift for herself, I can only plead the necessity of the case. Stay where he was he could not; go he must at any rate: I trundled him off in the best way that I could; and, for the sake of the public, I heartily wish that way had been better. With regard to his not meeting Osmond in his flight, a little imagination will soon conquer that difficulty. It may be supposed, that as he lost his way in coming, he lost it again in going; or, that he concealed himself till the Earl had passed him; or, that he tumbled down and broke his neck; or, that he . . . did any thing else you like better. I leave this matter entirely to the reader's fancy.

Against my Spectre many objections have been urged: one of them I think rather curious. She ought not to appear, because the belief in Ghosts no longer exists! In my opinion, that is the very reason why she may be produced without danger; for there is now no fear of increasing the influence of superstition, or strengthening the prejudices of the weak-minded. I confess I cannot see any reason why Apparitions may not be as well permitted to stalk in a tragedy, as Fairies be suffered to fly in a pantomime, or Heathen Gods and Goddesses to cut capers in a grand ballet; and I should rather imagine that Oberon and Bacchus now find as little credit to the full as the Cock-lane Ghost, or the Spectre of Mrs. Veal.

Never was any poor soul so ill-used as Evelina's, previous to her presenting herself before the audience. The Friends to whom I read my Drama, the Managers to whom I presented it, the Actors who were to perform in it – all combined to persecute my Spectre, and requested me to confine my Ghost to the greenroom. Aware that without her my catastrophe would closely resemble that of the Grecian Daughter, I persisted in retaining her. The event justified my obstinacy: The Spectre was as well treated before the curtain as she had been ill-used behind it; and as she continues to make her appearance nightly with increased applause, I think myself under great obligations both to her and her representative.

But though I am conscious that it is very imperfect, I shall not so far offend my own feelings, or insult the judgment of the public, which has given it a very favourable reception, as to say that I think my Play very bad. Had such been my opinion, instead of producing it on the stage, or committing it to the press, I should have put it behind the fire, or, throwing it into the Thames, made a present of it to the British Scombri. Still its success on the stage (great enough to content even an author) does not prevent my being very doubtful as to its reception in the closet, when divested of its beautiful music, splendid scenery, and, above all, of the acting, excellent throughout. Without detracting from the merits of the other performers (to all of whom I think myself much indebted for their respective exertions), I must here be permitted to return particular thanks to Mrs. Jordan, whose manner of sustaining her character exceeded my most sanguine hopes, and in whose hands my heroine acquired an importance for which she was entirely indebted to the talents of the actress.

M.G. LEWIS.

DRAMATIS PERSONAE.

Osmond, Mr. Barrymore.
Reginald, Mr. Wroughton.
Percy, Mr. Kemble.
Father Philip, Mr. Palmer.
Motley, Mr. Bannister, Jun.
Kenric, Mr. Aickin.
Saib, Mr. Truman.
Hassan, Mr. Dowton.
Muley, Mr. Davis.
Alaric, Mr. Wentworth.
Allan, Mr. Packer.
Edric, Mr. Wathen.
Harold, Mr. Gibbon

Angela, Mrs. Jordan.
Alice, Mrs. Walcot.
Evelina, Mrs. Powell.

ACT I

SCENE I. – A Grove

Enter Father Philip and Motley.

F. PHIL: Never tell me! – I repeat it, you are a fellow of a very scandalous course of life!

MOTL: And I repeat it, I'm a perfect image of the purest virtue, compared to whom, for sobriety and continence, Cato was a drunkard, and Lucretia little better than she should be.

F. PHIL: Oh! hardened in impudence! – Can you deny being a pilferer, a lyar, a glutton–

MOTL: Can I? – Heaven be thanked, I've courage enough to deny any thing!

F. PHIL: Doesn't all the world cry out upon you?

MOTL: Certainly my transcendant merit has procured me some enemies, and, in common with many other great men, my virtue at present labours under something of a cloud. But understand me right, Father: Though I don't assent to the sum-total of your accusations, possibly I may acknowledge some of the items; the best actions frequently appear culpable, merely because their motives are unexplained. Therefore produce your charges, let me justify my conduct, and I doubt not I shall retrieve my reputation from your hands as immaculate and pure as a new sheet of foolscap.

F. PHIL: To begin then with your pilfering – Did you, or did you not, break open the pantry-door, and steal out the great goose-pye?

MOTL: Begging your pardon, Father, that was no fault of mine.

F. PHIL: Whose then?

MOTL: The cook's undoubtedly; for if he hadn't locked the pantry-door, 'tis an hundred to one I shouldn't have taken the trouble to break it open.

F. PHIL: Nonsense! Nonsense! – I tell you, you've been guilty of stealing, which is a monstrous crime! And what did you steal? Had you taken any thing else I might have forgiven you: but to lay irreverent hands upon the goose-pye! – As I'm a Christian, the identical goose-pye which I intended for my own supper! – But this is not my only objection to your conduct.

MOTL: No?

F. PHIL: What principally offends me is, that you pervert the minds of the maids, and keep kissing and smuggling all the pretty girls you meet. Oh! fye! fye!

MOTL: I kiss and smuggle them? St. Francis forbid! Lord love you, Father, 'tis they who kiss and smuggle me. I protest I do what I can to preserve my modesty; and I wish that Archbishop Dunstan had heard the lecture upon chastity which I read last night to the dairymaid in the dark! he'd have been quite edified. But yet what does talking signify? The eloquence of my lips is counteracted by the lustre of my eyes; and really the little devils are so tender, and so troublesome, that I'm half angry with nature for having made me so very bewitching.

F. PHIL: Nonsense! Nonsense!

MOTL: Why it was but yesterday that Cicely and Luce went to fisty-cuffs, quarrelling which looked neatest-my red leg, or my yellow one. Then they are so fond and so coaxing! They hang about one so lovingly! And one says, 'Kind Mr. Motley!' and t'other, 'Sweet Mr. Motley!' – Ah! Father Philip! Father Philip! How is a poor little bit of flesh and blood, like me, to resist such temptation? – Put yourself in my place: Suppose that a sweet smiling rogue, just sixteen, with rosy cheeks, sparkling eyes, pouting lips, &c.

F.PHIL. Oh! fye! fye! fye! – To hear such licentious discourse brings the tears into my eyes!

MOTL: I believe you, Father; for I see the water is running over at your mouth. However, this shews you–

F. PHIL: It shews me that you are a reprobate, and that my advice is thrown away upon you: In future I shall keep those counsels to myself, which I offered you from motives of pure Christian charity.

MOTL: Charity, my good Father, should always begin at home: Now, instead of giving yourself so much trouble to mend me, what if you thought a little of correcting yourself?

F.PHIL. I? – I have nothing to correct.

MOTL: No, to be sure!

F. PHIL: The odour of my sanctity perfumes the whole kingdom.

MOTL: It has a powerful smell about it, I own, not unlike carrion; you may wind it a mile off.

F. PHIL: All malice!

MOTL: Not exactly: I could mention some little points which might be altered in you still better than in myself; such as intemperance, gluttony–

F. PHIL: Gluttony? – Oh! abominable falsehood!

MOTL: Plain matter of fact! – Why will any man pretend to say that you came honestly by that enormous belly, that tremendous tomb of fish, flesh, and fowl? I protest I'm grateful to Heaven that among the unclean Beasts who accompanied Noah, there went not into the ark a pair of fat monks: they must infallibly have created a famine, and then the world would never have been re-peopled. – Next, for incontinence, you must allow yourself that you are unequalled.

F. PHIL: I? I?

MOTL: You, You. – May I ask what was your business in the beech-grove the other evening, when I caught you with buxom Margery the miller's pretty wife? Was it quite necessary to lay your heads together so close?

F. PHIL: Perfectly necessary: I was whispering in her ear wholesome advice.

MOTL: Indeed? Faith then she took your advice as kindly as it was given, and exactly in the same way too: you gave it with your lips, and she took it with hers! – Well done, Father Philip!

F. PHIL: Son, Son, you give your tongue too great a licence.

MOTL: Nay, Father, be not angry: Fools, you know, are privileged persons.

F. PHIL: I know they are very useless ones; and in short, Master Motley, to be plain with you, of all fools I think you are the worst; and for fools of all kinds I've an insuperable aversion.

MOTL: Really? Then you have one good quality at least, and I cannot but admire such a total want of self-love!

(An horn sounds.) But hark! 'tis the dinner-horn. Away to table, Father – Depend upon't, the servants will rather eat part of their dinner unblessed, than stay till your stomach comes like Jonas's whale, and swallows up the whole.

F. PHIL: Well, well, fool, I am going: but first let me explain to you, that my bulk proceeds from no Indulgence of voracious appetite. No, son, no: Little sustenance do I take; but St. Cuthbert's blessing is upon me, and that little prospers with me most marvellously. Verily, the Saint has given me rather too plentiful an increase, and my legs are scarce able to support the weight of his bounties. (Exit)

MOTL: (Alone.) He looks like an overgrown turtle, waddling upon its hind fins! – Yet at bottom 'tis a good fellow enough, warmhearted, benevolent, friendly, and sincere; but no more intended by nature to be a monk, than I to be a maid of honour to the Queen of Sheba. (Going.)

Enter Percy.

PERCY: I cannot be mistaken: in spite of his dress, his features are too well known to me! Hist! Gilbert! Gilbert!

MOTL: Gilbert? Oh Lord, that's I! – Who calls?

PERCY: Have you forgotten me?

MOTL: Truly, sir, that would be no easy matter; I never forgot in my life what I never knew.

PERCY: Have ten years altered me so much that you cannot–

MOTL: Hey! – Can it be – Pardon, my dear master, pardon! – In truth, you may well forgive my having forgotten your name, for at first I didn't very well remember my own. However, to prevent further mistakes, I must inform you, that he who in your father's service was Gilbert the knave, is Motley the fool in the service of Earl Osmond.

PERCY: Of Earl Osmond? This is fortunate. Gilbert, you may be of use to me; and if the attachment which as a boy you professed for me still exists–

MOTL: It does with ardour unabated, for I'm not so unjust as to attribute to you my expulsion from Alnwic Castle: in fact I deserved it, for I cannot deny but that at twenty I was as good-for-nothing a knave as ever existed; consequently old Earl Percy dismissed me from his service, but I know that it was sorely against your inclination. You were then scarce fourteen, and I had been your companion and play-fellow from your childhood. I remember well your grief at parting with me, and that you slipped into my hand the purse which contained the whole of your little treasure. That act of kindness struck to my heart: I swore at the moment to love you through life, and if ever I forget my oath, damn me!

PERCY: My honest Gilbert! – And what made you assume this habit?

MOTL: Ah, my Lord! what could I do? – In spite of my knavery and tricks I was constantly upon the point of starving, and having once contracted an idle habit of eating, I never could bring myself to leave it off. After living five years by my wits, want drove me almost out of them: I knew not what course to take, when I heard that Earl Osmond's jester had fled the country. I exerted my knavery for the last time in stealing the fugitive's cast coat, was accepted in his place by the Earl, and now gain an honest livelihood by persuading my neighbours that I'm a greater fool than themselves.

PERCY: And your change is for the better?

MOTL: Infinitely; indeed your fool is universally preferred to your knave – and for this reason; your fool is cheated, your knave cheats: Now everybody had rather cheat, than be cheated.

PERCY: Some truth in that.

MOTL: And now, sir, may I ask, what brings you to Wales?

PERCY: A woman, whom I adore.

MOTL: Yes, I guessed that the business was about a petticoat. And this woman is–

PERCY: The orphan ward of a villager, without friends, without family, without fortune!

MOTL: Great points in her favour, I must confess. And which of these excellent qualities won your heart?

PERCY: I hope I had better reasons for bestowing it on her. No, Gilbert; I loved her for a person beautiful without art, and graceful without affectation – for an heart tender without weakness, and noble without pride. I saw her at once beloved and reverenced by her village companions: they looked on her as a being of a superior order; and I felt, that she who gave such dignity to the cottage-maid, must needs add new lustre to the coronet of the Percies.

MOTL: From which I am to understand that you mean to marry this rustic.

PERCY: Could I mean otherwise, I should blush for myself.

MOTL: Yet surely the baseness of her origin—

PERCY: Can to me be no objection: in giving her my hand I raise her to my station, not debase myself to hers; nor ever, while gazing on the beauty of a rose, did I think it less fair because planted by a peasant.

MOTL: Bravo! – And what says your good grumbling father to this?

PERCY: Alas! he has long slept in the grave!

MOTL: Then he's quiet at last! Well, God grant him that peace in heaven, which he suffered nobody to enjoy on earth! – But, his death having left you master of your actions, what obstacle now prevents your marriage?

PERCY: You shall hear. – Fearful lest my rank should influence this lovely girl's affections, and induce her to bestow her hand on the noble, while she refuses her heart to the man, I assumed a peasant's habit, and presented myself as Edwy the lowborn and the poor. In this character I gained her heart, and resolved to hail, as Countess of Northumberland, the betrothed of Edwy the lowborn and the poor!

MOTL: I warrant the pretty soul wasn't displeased with the discovery!

PERCY: That discovery is still unmade. Judge how great must have been my disappointment, when, on entering her guardian's cottage with this design, he informed me, that the unknown, who sixteen years before had confided her to his care, had reclaimed her on that very morning, and conveyed her no one knew whither.

MOTL: That was unlucky.

PERCY: Was it not? – Ah! had I declared myself one day sooner, ere this she would have been my wife.

MOTL: True; and being your wife, if a stranger then had conveyed her no one knew whither, you might have thought yourself mightily obliged to him.

PERCY: However, in spite of his precautions, I have traced the stranger's course, and find him to be Kenric, a dependent upon Earl Osmond.

MOTL: Surely 'tis not Lady Angela, who–

PERCY: The very same! Speak, my good fellow! Do you know her?

MOTL: Not by your description; for here she's understood to be the daughter of Sir Malcolm Mowbray, my master's deceased friend. And what is your present intention?

PERCY: To demand her of the Earl in marriage.

MOTL: Oh! – that will never do:– for in the first place you'll not be able to get a sight of him. I've now lived with him five long years, and, till Angela's arrival, never witnessed a guest in the Castle. – Oh! 'tis the most melancholy mansion! And as to its master, he's the very antidote to mirth: He always walks with his arms folded, his brows bent, his eyes louring on you with a gloomy scowl: He never smiles; and to laugh in his presence would be high treason. He looks at no one – speaks to no one. None dare approach him, except Kenric and his four blacks – all others are ordered to avoid him; and whenever he quits his room, ding! dong! goes a great bell, and away run the servants like so many scared rabbits.

PERCY: Strange! – and what reasons can he have for–

MOTL: Oh! reasons in plenty. You must know there's an ugly story respecting the last owners of this Castle – Osmond's brother, his wife, and infant child, were murdered by banditti, as it was said: unluckily the only servant who escaped the slaughter, deposed, that he recognized among the assassins a black still in the service of Earl Osmond. The truth of this assertion was never known, for the servant was found dead in his bed the next morning.

PERCY: Good heavens!

MOTL: Since that time no sound of joy has been heard in Conway Castle. Osmond instantly became gloomy and ferocious; he now never utters a sound except a sigh, has broken every tie of society, and keeps his gates barred unceasingly against the stranger.

PERCY: Yet Angela is admitted:– But, no doubt, affection for her father–

MOTL: Why, no; I rather think that affection for her father's child–

PERCY: How?

MOTL: If I've any knowledge in love, the Earl feels it for his fair ward: But the Lady will tell you more of this, if I can procure for you an interview.

PERCY: That very request which–

MOTL: 'Tis no easy matter, I promise you; but I'll do my best. In the meanwhile wait for me in yonder fishing hut – its owner's name is Edric; – tell him that I sent you, and he will give you a retreat.

PERCY: Farewell, then, and remember that whatever reward–

MOTL: Dear master, to mention a reward insults me. You have already shown me kindness; and when 'tis in my power to be of use to you, to need the inducement of a second favour would prove me a scoundrel undeserving of the first. (Exit)

PERCY: How warm is this good fellow's attachment! Yet our Barons complain that the great can have no friends! If they have none, let their own pride bear the blame. Instead of looking with scorn on those whom a smile would attract, and a favour bind for ever, how many firm friends might our nobles gain, if they would but reflect that their vassals are men as they are, and have hearts whose feelings can be grateful as their own. (Exit)

***

SCENE II. – The Castle-Hall.

Saib and Hassan meeting.

SAIB: Now, Hassan, what success?

HASS: My search has been fruitless. In vain have I paced the river's banks, and pierced the grove's deepest recesses. Nor glen nor thicket have I passed unexplored, yet found no stranger to whom Kenric's description could apply.

SAIB: Saw you no one?

HASS: A troop of horsemen passed me as I left the wood.

SAIB: Horsemen, say you? – Then Kenric may be right. Earl Percy has discovered Angela's abode, and lurks near the Castle in hopes of carrying her off.

HASS: His hopes then will be vain. Osmond's vigilance will not easily be eluded – sharpened by those powerful motives, love and fear.

SAIB: His love, I know; but should he lose Angela, what has he to fear?

HASS: If Percy gains her, every thing! Supported by such wealth and power, dangerous would be her claim to these domains should her birth be discovered. Of this our Lord is aware; nor did he sooner hear that Northumberland loved her, than he hastened to remove her from Allan's care. At first I doubt his purpose was a foul one: her resemblance to her mother induced him to change it. He now is resolved to make her his bride, and restore to her those rights of which himself deprived her.

SAIB: Think you the Lady perceives that our Master loves her?

HASS: I know she does not. Absorbed in her own passion for Percy, on Osmond's she bestows no thought, and, while roving through these pompous halls and chambers, sighs for the Cheviot Hills, and Allan's humble cottage.

SAIB: But as she still believes Percy to be a lowborn swain, when Osmond lays his coronet at her feet, will she reject his rank and splendour?

HASS: If she loves well, she will. Saib, I too have loved! I have known how painful it was to leave her on whom my heart hung; how incapable was all else to supply her loss! I have exchanged want for plenty, fatigue for rest, a wretched hut for a splendid palace. But am I happier? Oh! no! Still do I regret my native land, and the partners of my poverty. Then toil was sweet to me, for I laboured for Samba; then repose ever bless'd my bed of leaves, for there by my side lay Samba sleeping.

SAIB: This from you, Hassan? – Did love ever find a place in your flinty bosom?

HASS: Did it? Oh Saib! my heart once was gentle, once was good! But sorrows have broken it, insults have made it hard! I have been dragged from my native land, from a wife who was every thing to me, to whom I was every thing! Twenty years have elapsed since these Christians tore me away: they trampled upon my heart, mocked my despair, and, when in frantic terms I raved of Samba, laughed, and wondered how a negro's soul could feel! In that moment when the last point of Africa faded from my view, when as I stood on the vessel's deck I felt that all I loved was to me lost for ever, in that bitter moment did I banish humanity from my breast. I tore from my arm the bracelet of Samba's hair, I gave to the sea the precious token, and, while the high waves swift bore it from me, vowed aloud endless hatred to mankind. I have kept my oath, I will keep it!

SAIB: Ill-starred Hassan! your wrongs have indeed been great.

HASS: To remember them unmans me – Farewell! I must to Kenric. Hold! – Look, where he comes from Osmond's chamber!

SAIB: And seemingly in wrath.

HASS: His conferences with the Earl of late have had no other end. The period of his favour is arrived.

SAIB: Not of his favour merely, Hassan.

HASS: How? Mean you that...

SAIB: His anxiety for independence, his wish to withdraw himself from Wales – yet more, certain mysterious words and threats for some time past have made our Lord uneasy. By him was I this morning commissioned· Silence! He's here! you shall know more anon.

Enter Kenric.

KENR: His promise ever evaded! My request still heard with impatience, and treated with neglect. – Osmond, I will bear your ingratitude no longer. – Now, Hassan, found you the man described?

HASS: Nor any that resembled him.

KENR: Yet, that I saw Percy, I am convinced. As I crossed him in the wood, his eye met mine. He started as had he seen a basilisk, and fled with rapidity. Be on your guard, my friends! Doubtless he will attempt to gain admission to the Castle.

HASS: Can we be otherwise than watchful, when we see how well the Earl rewards his followers?

SAIB: Of that, Kenric, you are an example. Have you obtained that recompense so long promised? Do you enjoy that independence which...

KENR: Saib, the Earl's ingratitude cuts me to the heart! Attached to him from his infancy, I have long been his friend, long fancied him mine. The illusion is now over. He sees that I can serve him no further – knows that I can harm him much; therefore he fears, and, fearing, hates me! But I will submit no longer to this painful dependence. tomorrow, for the last time, will I summon him to perform his promise: If he refuses, I will bid him farewell for ever, and, by my absence, free him from a restraint equally irksome to myself and him.

SAIB: Will you so, Kenric? – Be speedy then, or you will be too late.

KENR: Too late! And wherefore?

SAIB: You will soon receive the reward of your services.

KENR: Ha! Know you what that reward will be?

SAIB: I guess, but may not tell.

KENR: Is it a secret?

SAIB: Can you keep one?

KENR: Faithfully!

SAIB: As faithfully can I. Come, Hassan. (Exeunt)

KENR: (Alone.) What meant the slave? Those doubtful expressions . . . Ha! should the Earl intend me false . . . Kenric! Kenric! how is thy nature changed! There was time when fear was a stranger to my bosom – when, guiltless myself, I dreaded not art in others. Now, where'er I turn me, danger appears to lurk; and I suspect treachery in every breast, because my own heart hides it. (Exit)

Enter Father Philip, followd by Alice.

F. PHIL: Nonsense! – You silly woman, what you say is not possible.

ALICE: I never said it was possible. I only said it was true; and that if ever I heard music, I heard it last night.

F. PHIL: Perhaps the fool was singing to the servants.

ALICE: The fool indeed? Oh! fye! fye! How dare you call my Lady's ghost a fool?

F. PHIL: Your Lady's ghost! – You silly old woman!

ALICE: Yes, Father, yes: I repeat it, I heard the guitar lying upon the Oratory table play the very air which the Lady Evelina used to sing while rocking her little daughter's cradle. She warbled it so sweetly, and ever at the close it went (Singing.)

'Lullaby! Lullaby! hush thee, my dear!

'Thy father is coming, and soon will be here!'

F. PHIL: Nonsense! nonsense! – Why, pr'ythee, Alice, do you think that your Lady's ghost would get up at night only to sing Lullaby for your amusement? – Besides, how should a spirit, which is nothing but air, play upon an instrument of material wood and cat gut?

ALICE: How can I tell? – Why, I know very well that men are made; but if you desired me to make a man, I vow and protest I shouldn't know how to set about it. I can only say, that last night I heard the ghost of my murdered Lady...

F. PHIL: Playing upon the spirit of a cracked guitar! – Alice! Alice! these fears are ridiculous! The idea of ghosts is a vulgar prejudice; and they who are timid and absurd enough to encourage it, prove themselves the most contemptible–

ALICE: (Screaming.) Oh! Lord bless us!

F. PHIL: What? – Hey! – Oh! dear!

ALICE: Look! look! – A figure in white! – It comes from the haunted room!

F. PHIL: (Dropping on his knees.) Blessed St. Patrick! – Who has got my beads? Where's my prayer-book?

ALICE: It comes! – it comes! – Now! now! – Lack-a-day, it's only Lady Angela!

F. PHIL: (Rising) Lack-a-day! I'm glad of it with all my heart!

ALICE: Truly so am I. – But what say you now, Father, to the fear of spectres!

F. PHIL: In good faith, Alice, that my theory was better than my practice. However, the next time that you are afraid of a ghost, remember and make use of the receipt which I shall now give you; instead of calling for a priest to lay the spirits of other people in the red sea, call for a bottle of red wine to raise your own. Probatum est (Exit)

ALICE: (Alone.) Wine indeed! – I believe he thinks I like drinking as well as himself. No, no! Let the old toping friar take his bottle of wine; I shall confine myself to plain cherry-brandy.

Enter Angela.

ANG: I am weary of wandering from room to room; in vain do I change the scene, discontent is every where. There was a time when music could delight my ear, and nature could charm my eye:– when, as the dawn unveiled the landscape, each object it disclosed to me looked pleasant and fair; and while the last sunbeams yet lingered on the western sky, I could pour forth a prayer of gratitude, and thank my good angels for a day unclouded by sorrow! – Now all is gone, all lost, all faded!

ALICE: Lady!

ANG: Perhaps at this moment he thinks upon me! Perhaps he wanders on those mountains where we so oft have strayed, reclines on that bank where we so oft have sat, or listens sadly to the starling which he taught to repeat my name. Perhaps then he sighs, and murmurs to himself, 'The flowers, the rivulets, the birds, every object reminds me of my well-beloved; but what shall remind her of Edwy?' – Oh! that will my heart, Edwy; I need no other remembrancer!

ALICE: Lady! Lady Angela! – She minds me no more than a post!

ANG: Oh! are you there, good Alice? What would you with me?

ALICE: Only ask, how your Ladyship rested?

ANG: Ill! very ill!

ALICE: Lack-a-day! and yet you sleep in the best bed!

ANG: True, good Alice; but my heart's anguish strewed thorns upon my couch of down.

ALICE: Marry, I'm not surprised that you rested ill in the Cedar-room. Those noises so near you–

ANG: What noises? I heard none.

ALICE: How? – When the clock struck one, heard you no music?

ANG: Music! – None.

ALICE: And never have heard any while in the Cedar-room?

ANG: Not that I – Stay! now I remember that while I sat alone in my chamber this morning–

ALICE: Well, Lady, well!

ANG: Methought I heard some one singing; it seemed as if the words ran thus – (Singing.) – 'Lullaby! Lullaby! hush thee, my dear!'

ALICE: (Screaming.) The very words! – It was the ghost, Lady! it was the ghost!

ANG: The ghost, Alice! – I protest I thought it had been you.

ALICE: Me, Lady! – Lord, when did you hear this singing?

ANG: Not five minutes ago, while you were talking with Father Philip.

ALICE: The Lord be thanked! – Then it was not the ghost. It was I, Lady! It was I! – And have you heard no other singing since you came to the Castle?

ANG: None. But why that question?

ALICE: Because, Lady – But perhaps you may be frightened?

ANG: No, no! – Proceed, I entreat you!

ALICE: Why, then, they do say, that the chamber in which you sleep is haunted. You may have observed two folding-doors, which are kept locked: they lead to the Oratory, in which the Lady Evelina passed most of her time, while my Lord was engaged in the Scottish wars. She would sit there, good soul! hour after hour, playing on the lute, and singing airs so sweet, so sad, that many a time and oft have I wept to hear her. Ah! when I kissed her hand at the Castle-gate, little did I suspect that her fate would have been so wretched!

ANG: And what was her fate?

ALICE: A sad one, Lady! Impatient to embrace her Lord, after a year's absence, the Countess set out to met him on his return from Scotland, accompanied by a few domestics and her infant-daughter, then scarce a twelvemonth old. But, as she returned with her husband, robbers surprised the party scarce a mile from the Castle; and since that time no news has been received of the Earl, of the Countess, the servants, or the child.

ANG: Dreadful! Were not their corses found?

ALICE: Never! The only domestic who escaped pointed out the scene of action; and as it proved to be on the river's banks, doubtless the assassins plunged the bodies into the stream.

ANG: Strange! And did Earl Osmond then become owner of this Castle? – Alice! was he ever suspected of–

ALICE: Speak lower, Lady! It was said so, I own: but for my own part I never believed it. To my certain knowledge Osmond loved the Lady Evelina too well to hurt her; and when he heard of her death, he wept, and sobbed as if his heart were breaking. Nay, 'tis certain that he proposed to her before marriage, and would have made her his wife, only that she liked his brother better. Well she might indeed, for Earl Reginald was a sweeter gentleman by half.

ANG: And in that Oratory, you say – Good Alice, you have the key of it: Let me see that Oratory tonight.

ALICE: tonight, Lady? Heaven preserve me! I wouldn't enter it after dark for the world!

ANG: But before dark, Alice?

ALICE: Before dark? Why that indeed – Well, well, we'll see, Lady. But I hope you're not alarmed by what I mentioned of the Cedar-room?

ANG: No, truly, Alice; from good spirits I have nothing to fear, and heaven and my innocence will protect me against bad.

ALICE: My very sentiments, I protest! But Heaven forgive me, while I stand gossiping here I warrant all goes wrong in the kitchen! Your pardon, Lady: I must away! I must away! (Exit)

ANG: (Musing.) Osmond was his brother's heir. His strange demeanour! – Yes, in that gloomy brow is written a volume of villainy! Heavenly powers! an assassin then is master of my fate! – An assassin too who – I dare not bend my thoughts that way! – Oh! would I had never entered these Castle-walls! – had never exchanged for fearful pomp the security of my pleasures – the tranquillity of my soul!

> Return, return, sweet Peace! and o'er my breast
> Spread thy bright wings, distil thy balmy rest,
> And teach my steps thy realms among to rove;
> Wealth and the world resign'd, nought mine but love!
> Ah! cease thy suit, fond girl! thy prayer is vain,
> For thus did Love his tyrant law ordain.
> – 'Peace still must fly that heart where I still reign.'

(Exit)

END OF THE FIRST ACT

ACT II

SCENE I. – The Armoury. – Suits of Armour are arranged on both Sides upon Pedestals, with the Names of their Possessors written under each.

Enter Motley, peeping in.

MOTL: The coast is clear! – Hist! Hist! – You may enter.

Enter Percy.

PERCY: Loiter not here! – Quick, my good fellow! – Conduct me to Angela!

MOTL: Softly, softly! A little caution is needful; and I promise you just now I'm not upon roses. – You remember the servant who hinted that Earl Osmond had an hand in his brother's murder? – Should I be suspected of admitting you to the Castle, his fate might be mine; and whatever you may think of it, my Lord, I shouldn't be at all pleased at waking tomorrow morning, to find myself dead in my bed.

PERCY: If such are your fears, why not lead me at once to Angela? Are we not more exposed in this open hall?

MOTL: Be contented, and leave all to me: I will contrive matters so that Osmond shall have you before his eyes, and be no jot the wiser. – Here! – (Taking down a suit of armour) – Put on this coat of mail: you must make up your mind to play a statue for an hour or two.

PERCY: How?

MOTL: Nay, 'tis absolutely necessary. – Quick! quick! ere the servants quit the hall, where they are now at dinner. – Here's the helmet! – the gauntlet! – the shield! – So now take this truncheon in your hand; and there we have you armed cap-a-pee!

PERCY: And now be good enough to explain what purpose this masquerade is to answer.

MOTL: Willingly. You are to know, that since the late Earl's death the Castle is thought to be haunted: the servants are fully persuaded that his ghost wanders every night through the long galleries, and parades the old towers and dreary halls which abound in this melancholy mansion. He is supposed to be drest in compleat armour; and that which you wear at present was formerly his. Now hear my plan. The Earl prepares to hold a conference with Lady Angela; even now I heard her summoned to attend him in the Armoury. Placed upon this pedestal you may listen to their discourse unobserved, and thus form a proper judgment both of your mistress and her guardian. As soon as it grows dark I will conduct you to Angela's apartments: the obscurity will then shelter you from discovery; and even should you be observed, you will pass for Earl Reginald's spectre.

PERCY: I do not dislike your plan: but tell me, Gilbert, do you believe this tale of the apparition?

MOTL: Oh! Heaven forbid! Not a word of it. Had I minded all the strange things related of this Castle, I should have died of fright in the first half-hour. Why, they say that Earl Hubert rides every night round the Castle on a white horse; that the ghost of Lady Bertha haunts the west pinnacle of the Chapel-Tower; and that Lord Hildebrand, who was condemned for treason some sixty years ago, may be seen in the Great Hall, regularly at midnight, playing at football with his own head! Above all, they say that the spirit of the late Countess sits nightly in her Oratory, and sings her baby to sleep! However, if it be so – (A bell sounds thrice, loud and solemn.) – Hark! 'tis the Earl! – Quick to your post!–

(Percy ascends the pedestal.)

– Farewell! I must get out of his way; but as soon as he quits this chamber I'll rejoin you.

PERCY: Do so; and farewell. (Exit Motley)

(The folding-doors are thrown open: Saib, Hassan, Muley, and Alaric enter, preceding Earl Osmond, who walks with his arms folded, and his eyes bent upon the ground. Saib advances a sopha, into which, after making a few turns through the room, Osmond throws himself. He motions to his attendants, and they withdraw. He appears lost in thought; then suddenly rises, and again traverses the room with disordered steps.)

OSM: I will not sacrifice my happiness to hers! For sixteen long years have I thirsted; and now when the cup of joy again stands full before me, shall I dash it from my lip? No, Angela, you ask of me too much. Since the moment when I pierced her heart, deprived of whom life became odious; since my soul was stained with his blood who loved me, with hers whom I loved, no form has been grateful to my eye, no voice spoken pleasure to my soul, save Angela's, save only Angela's! Doting upon one whom death has long clasped in his arms;

tortured by desires which I never hoped to satisfy, many a mournful year has my heart known no throb but of anguish, no guest but remorse at committing a fruitless crime. Hope, that stranger, once more revisits my bosom: the fiend, who led me through passion's mazes to the heights of guilt, owns that a crime so great well merits a reward. He bids the monument's jaws unclose: Evelina revives in her daughter, and soon shall the fires which consume me be quenched in Angela's arms. What though her heart be Percy's? What though she prefers a basilisk's kiss to mine? Because my short-lived joy may cause her eternal sorrow, shall I reject those pleasures sought so long, desired so earnestly? That will I not, by Heaven! Mine she is, and mine she shall be, though Reginald's bleeding ghost flit before me, and thunder in my ear – 'Hold! Hold!' – Peace, stormy heart! She comes! (Enter Angela.)

OSM: (In a softened voice.) Come hither, Angela. Wherefore so sad? That downcast eye, that listless air, neither suit your age or fortunes. Raised from obscurity to rank and splendour, can this change call no smile upon your cheek? Where-e'er you turn, respect and adoration wait you; a thousand servants move obedient to your nod. The treasures of India are lavished to adorn your person; yet still do I see you, forgetting what you are, look back with regret to what you were!

ANG: Oh! my good Lord, esteem me not ungrateful! I acknoledge your bounties, but they have not made me happy. I still linger in thought near those scenes where I passed the blessed period of infancy; I still thirst for those simple pleasures which habit has made to me most dear. The birds which my own hands reared, and the flowers which my own hands planted; the banks on which

I rested when fatigued, the wild tangled wood which supplied me with strawberries, and the village church where I prayed to be virtuous, while I yet knew of vice and virtue but the name, all have acquired rights to my memory and my love!

OSM: What? these costly dresses, these scenes of pomp and greatness–

ANG: Dazzle my eyes, but leave my heart unsatisfied. What I would meet with is affection, not respect; I had rather be obliged than obeyed; and all these glittering gems are far less dear to me, than one flower of a wreath which Edwy's hands have woven.

OSM: Confusion!

ANG: While I saw you, Cheviot Hills, I was happy, Oh! how happy! While I listened to your artless accents, friends of my childhood, how swelled my fond heart with gratitude and pleasure. At morn when I left my bed, light were my spirits, and gay as the zephyrs of summer; and when at night my head again pressed my pillow, I whispered to myself, 'Happy has been today, and tomorrow will be as happy!' Then sweet was my sleep; and my dreams were of those whom I loved dearest.

OSM: Romantic enthusiast! These thoughts did well for the village maid, but disgrace the daughter of Sir Malcolm Mowbray: Let them be changed for others, better suited to your birth, to the fortune which awaits you. Hear me, Angela; an English baron loves you, a nobleman than whom our island boasts few more potent. 'Tis to him that your hand is destined, 'tis on him that your heart must be bestowed.

ANG: I cannot dispose of that which has long been another's – My heart is Edwy's.

OSM: Edwy's? A peasant's?

ANG: For the obscurity of his birth chance must be blamed; the merit of his virtues belongs wholly to himself.

OSM: By Heaven, you seem to think that poverty is a virtue!

ANG: Sir, I think 'tis a misfortune, not a crime: And when in spite of' nature's injustice, and the frowns of a prejudiced and illiberal world, I see some lowborn but illustrious spirit prove itself superior to the station which it fills, I hail it with pleasure, with admiration, with respect! Such a spirit I found in Edwy, and, finding, loved!

OSM: My blood boils with passion!

ANG: You say, that by these sentiments I disgrace my rank: I say, that to break my given word would disgrace it more. Edwy has my plighted faith: He received it on the last evening which I passed in Northumberland, as we sat on a low bench before old Allan's cottage. It was an heavenly night, sweet and tranquil as the loves of angels: A gentle breeze whispered among the honeysuckles which bloomed above us, and the full moon tinged with her silver light the distant towers of Alnwic. It was then that for the first time I gave him my hand, and I swore that I never would give it but to him! It was then that for the first time he pressed his lips to mine, and I swore that my lips should never by pressed by another!

OSM: Girl! girl! you drive me to distraction!

ANG: You alarm me, my Lord! Permit me to retire. – (Going, Osmond detains her violently by the arm.)

OSM: Stay! – (In a softer tone.) Angela! I love you!

ANG: (Starting.) My Lord!

OSM: (Passionately.) Love you to madness! – My bosom is a gulph of devouring flames! I must quench them in your arms, or perish! – Nay, strive not to escape: Remain, and hear me! I offer you my hand: If you accept it, mistress of these fair and rich domains, your days shall glide away in happiness and honour; but if you refuse and scorn my offer, force shall this instant–

ANG: Force? Oh! No! – You dare not be so base!

OSM: Reflect on your situation, Angela; you are in my power – remember it, and be wise!

ANG: If you have a generous mind, that will be my surest safeguard. Be it my plea, Osmond, when thus I sue to you for mercy, for protection! Look on me with pity, Osmond! 'Tis the daughter of the man you loved, 'tis a creature, friendless, wretched, and forlorn, who kneels before you, who flies to you for refuge! True, I am in your power: Then save me, respect me, treat me not cruelly; for – I am in your power!

OSM: I will hear no more. Will you accept my offer?

ANG: Osmond, I conjure you–

OSM: Answer my question!

ANG: Mercy! Mercy!

OSM: Will you be mine? – Speak! Speak!

ANG: (After a moment's pause, rises, and pronounces with firmness.) Never, so help me Heaven!

OSM: (Seizing her.) Your fate then is decided!

(Angela shrieks.)

PERCY: (In a hollow voice.) – Hold!

OSM: (Starts, but still grasps Angela's arm.) – Ha! What was that?

ANG: (Struggling to escape.) Hark! Hark! – Heard you not a voice?

OSM: (Gazing upon Percy.) – It came from hence! – From Reginald! – Was it not a delusion? – Did indeed his spirit – (Relapsing into his former passion.) Well, be it so! Though his ghost should rush between us, thus would I clasp her – Horror! What sight is this! – (At the moment that he again seizes Angela, Percy extends his truncheon with a menacing gesture, and descends from the pedestal. Osmond releases Angela, who immediately rushes from the chamber, while Percy advances a few steps, and remains gazing on the Earl steadfastly.) – I know that shield! – that helmet! Speak to me, dreadful vision! – Tax me with my crimes! – Tell me, that you come – Stay! Speak! – (Following Percy, who, when he reaches the door, through which Angela escaped, turns, and signs to him with his hand. Osmond starts back in terror.)

– He forbids my following! – He leaves me! – The door closes – (In a sudden burst of passion, and drawing his sword.) – Hell, and fiends! I'll follow him, though lightnings blast me! – (He rushes distractedly from the chamber.)[1]

***

SCENE II. – *The Castle-Hall.*

Enter Alice.

ALICE: Here's rudeness! Here's ill-breeding! On my conscience, this house grows worse and worse every day!

Enter Motley.

MOTL: What can he have done with himself? Perhaps weary of waiting for me in the Armoury, he has found his way alone to Angela. How now, dame Alice, what has happened to you? You look angry.

---

[1] When I wrote the foregoing scene, I really believed the invention to be entirely my own: But the situations of Angela, Osmond and Percy, so closely resemble those of Isabella, Manfred, and the animated portrait in The Castle of Otranto, that I am convinced the idea must have been suggested to me by that beautiful Romance. – Wherever I can trace any plagiarisms, whether wilful or involuntary, I shall continue to point them out to the reader without reserve.

ALICE: By my troth, fool, I've little reason to look pleased. To be frightened out of my wits by night, and thumped and bumped about by day, is not likely to put one in the best humour.

MOTL: Poor soul! And who has been thumping and bumping you?

ALICE: Who has? You should rather ask who has not. – Why only hear:– As I was just now going along the narrow passage which leads to the Armoury – singing to myself, and thinking of nothing, I met Lady Angela flying away as if for dear life! – So I dropp'd her a curtsey – but might as well have spared my pains. Without minding me any more than if I had been a dog or a cat – she pushed me on one side: and before I could recover my balance, somebody else, who came bouncing by me, gave me t'other thump – and there I lay sprawling upon the floor. However, I tumbled with all possible decency, and took great care that my petticoats should cover my legs.

MOTL: Somebody else! What somebody else?

ALICE: I know not – but he seemed to be in armour.

MOTL: In armour? Pray, Alice, looked he like a ghost?

ALICE: What he looked like, I cannot say; – but I'm sure he didn't feel like one: However, you've not heard the worst. While I was sprawling upon the ground, my Lord comes tearing along the passage – The first thing he did was to stumble against me – away went his heels – over he came – and in the twinkling of an eye there lay his Lordship! As soon as he got up again – Mercy! how he stormed! – He snatched me up – called me an ugly old wirtch – shook the breath out of my body – then clapped me on the ground again, and bounced away after the other two!

MOTL: My mind misgives me! – But what can this mean, Alice?

ALICE: The meaning I neither know, or care about; – but this I know – I'll stay no longer in an house where I'm treated so disrespectfully. 'My Lady' – says I – 'Out of my way!' – says she, and pushes me on one side. – 'My Lord!' – says I – 'You be damned!' – says he, and pushes me on t'other! – I protest I never was so ill used, even when I was a young woman! (Exit)

MOTL: This account alarms me! – Should Percy be discovered – The very thought gives me a creak in my neck! – At any rate I had better enquire whether – (Going)

Enter Father Philip hastily.

F. PHIL: (Stopping him.) Get out of the house! – That's your way!

MOTL: Why, what's the meaning–

F. PHIL: Don't stand prating there, but do as I bid you!

MOTL: But first tell me–

F. PHIL: I can only tell you to get out of the house. Kenric has discovered Earl Percy – You are known to have introduced him – The Africans are in search of you

– If you are found, you will be hung out of hand. Fly then to Edric's cottage – hide yourself there! – Hark – Some one comes! Away, away, ere it is too late! – (Pushing him out)

MOTL: (Confused) But Earl Percy – But Angela–

F. PHIL: Leave them to me! You shall hear from me soon. Only take care of yourself, and fly with all diligence! – Away! (Exit Motley)

F. PHIL: (Alone.) So, so, he's off, and now I've time to take breath. I've not moved so nimbly for the last twenty years; and, in truth, I'm at present but ill calculated for velocity of motion. However, my exertions have not been thrown away: I've saved this poor knave from Osmond's vengeance – and should my plan for the Lady's release succeed – Poor little soul! – To see how she took on, when Percy was torn from her! Well, well, she shall be rescued from her tyrant. The moveable pannels – the subterraneous passages – the secret springs well-known to me – Oh! I cannot fail of success: But in order to secure it, I'll finally arrange my ideas in the Buttery. Whenever I've any great design in hand, I always ask advice of a flaggon of ale, and mature my plan over a cold venison-pasty. Oh! what an excellent genius must that man have had, who first invented eating and drinking! (Exit.)

***

SCENE III. – *A spacious Chamber: On one Side is a Couch: on the other a Table, which is placed under an arched and lofty Window.*

Enter Osmond, followed by Saib, Hassan, Muley and Alaric, who conduct Percy disarmed.

OSM: This, Sir, is your prison; but, doubtless, your confinement will not continue long. The moment which gives me Angela's hand shall restore you to liberty; and till that moment arrives, farewell.

PERCY: Stay, Sir, and hear me! – By what authority presume you to call me captive! – Have you forgotten that you speak to Northumberland's Earl?

OSM: Well may I forget him, who could so far forget himself. Was it worthy of Northumberland's Earl to steal disguised into my Castle, and plot with my servant to rob me of my most precious treasure?

PERCY: Mine was that treasure – You deprived me of it basely, and I was justified in striving to regain my own.

OSM: Earl, nothing can justify unworthy means. If you were wronged, why sought you not your right with your sword's point? I then should have esteemed you a noble foe, and as such would have treated you: But you have stooped to paltry artifice, and attacked me like some midnight ruffian, privately, and in disguise. By this am I authorized to forget your station, and make your penance as degrading as your offence was base.

PERCY: If such are indeed your sentiments, prove them now. Restore my sword, unsheathe your own, and be Angela the conqueror's reward!

OSM: No, Earl Percy! – I am not so rash a gamester as to suffer that cast to be recalled, by which the stake is mine already. Angela is in my power: The only man who could wrest her from my arms, has wilfully made himself my captive: Such he is, and such he shall remain.

PERCY: Insulting tyrant! Your cowardice in refusing my challenge proves sufficiently–

OSM: Be calm, Earl Percy! – You forget yourself. That I am no coward, my sword has proved in the fields of Scotland. – My sword shall again prove it, if, when you are restored to liberty, you still question the courage of my heart! Angela once mine, repeat your defiance, nor doubt my answering.

PERCY: Angela thine? – That she shall never be! There are angels above who favour virtue, and the hour of retribution must one day arrive! – (Throws himself upon the couch.)

OSM: But long ere the arrival of that hour shall Angela have been my bride; and now farewell, Lord Percy! – Muley and Saib!

BOTH. My Lord!

OSM: To your charge I commit the Earl; quit not his apartment, nor suffer him for one moment from your sight.

SAIB AND MULEY: My Lord, we shall obey you.

OSM: (Aside.) If she refuse me still, the death of this, her favourite – his death! Oh! through what bloody paths do I wander in pursuit of happiness! Yes, I am guilty! – Heaven! how guilty! Yet lies the fault with me? Did my own pleasure plant in my bosom these tempestuous passions? No! they were given me at my birth; they were sucked in with my existence! Nature formed me the slave of wild desires; and Fate, as she frowned upon my cradle, exclaimed, 'I doom this babe to be a villain and a wretch!'[2]

(Exit, followed by Hassan and Alaric, who lock the door after them.)

SAIB: Look, Muley, how bitterly he frowns!

MULEY: Now he starts from the sopha! – 'Faith, he's in a monstrous fury!

SAIB: That may well be:– When you mean to take in other people, it certainly is provoking to be taken in yourself.

PERCY: (After walking a few turns with a disordered air, suddenly stops.) He is gone to Angela! Gone, perhaps, to renew that outrage whose completion my presence alone prevented! Helpless and unprotected, with no friend but innocence – no advocates save tears – how will she now repel his violence?

---

[2] Having had good opportunities of knowing how wonderful are the talents for misinterpretation possessed by certain persons, I think it necessary to observe to my readers, that the foregoing speech is not meant to contain a moral sentiment, but to display the false reasoning of a guilty conscience. – If I were not to make this explanation, I should expect to see it asserted that the whole Play was meant to inculcate the doctrine of Fatality.

MULEY: Now he's in a deep study:- Marry, if he studies himself out of this Tower, he's a cleverer fellow than I take him for.

PERCY: Were I not Osmond's captive, all might yet be well. Summoning my vassals, who by this time must be near at hand, forcing the Castle, and tearing Angela from the arms of her tyrant – Alas! my captivity has rendered his plan impracticable! Eternal curses upon Gilbert, who persuaded me to adopt this artifice! – Curses on my own rash folly, which has thrown me thus defenceless in the power of my foe!–

MULEY: That's right! – Another stamp or two, and the Tower comes rattling about our ears.

PERCY: And are there then no hopes of liberty?

SAIB: He fixes his eyes on us.

PERCY: Might not these fellows – I can but try. – Now stand my friend, thou master-key to human hearts! – Aid me, thou potent devil, gold! – Hear me, my worthy friends! – Come nearer!

SAIB: His worthy friends! Are we such, Muley?

MULEY: Yes, truly we are – for friends in need are friends indeed – Marry, if he were not in need, he would call us his mortal foes.

PERCY: My, good fellows, you are charged with a disagreeable office, and to obey a tyrant's mandates cannot be pleasant to you; there is something in

your looks which has prejudiced me too much in your favour to believe it possible.

SAIB: Nay, there certainly is something in our appearance highly prepossessing.

MULEY: And I knew that you must admire the delicacy of our complexions!

PERCY: The tincture of your skin, my good fellow, is of little consequence: Many a worthy heart beats within a dusky bosom, and I am convinced that such an heart inhabits yours; for your looks tell me that you feel for, and are anxious to relieve, my sufferings. – See you this purse, my friends?

MULEY: It's too far off, and I'm shortsighted. – If you'll put it a little nearer–

PERCY: Restore me to liberty! – and not this purse alone, but ten times its value shall be yours.

SAIB: To liberty?

MULEY: That purse?

SAIB: Muley!

MULEY: Saib!

PERCY: (Aside.) By all my hopes, they hesitate! – You well know, that my wealth and power are equal, not to say superior, to Earl Osmond's:– Release me from my dungeon, and share that power and wealth! – On the events of today depends my life's future happiness, nay perhaps my life itself: Judge then, if you assist me, how great will be the service rendered me, and believe that your reward shall equal my obligation.

SAIB: I know not what to answer.

MULEY: In truth, my Lord, your offers are so generous, and that purse is so tempting – Saib, what say you? – (Winking to him.)

SAIB: The Earl speaks so well, and promises so largely, that I own I'm strangely tempted–

MULEY: Look you, Saib; will you stand by me?

SAIB: (After a moment's thought) I will!

MULEY: There's my hand then! – My Lord, we are your servants!

PERCY: This is beyond my hopes! – A thousand thanks, my worthy fellows! – Be assured that the performance of my promises shall soon follow the execution of yours.

SAIB: Of that we make no doubt.

PERCY: You agree then to release me?

MULEY: 'Tis impossible to do otherwise; for I feel that pity, generosity, and every moral feeling command me to trouble your Lordship for that purse.

PERCY: There it is! – And now unlock the door!

MULEY: (Chinking the purse.) Here it is! – And now I'm obliged to you. As for your promises, my Lord, pray don't trouble yourself to remember them, as I sha'n't trouble myself to remember mine.

PERCY: (Starting.) Ha! – What mean you?

SAIB: (Firmly.) Earl, that we are faithful!

MULEY: I wonder you didn't read that too in our amiable looks!

PERCY: What! Will you not keep your word?

MULFY. In good truth, No; we mean to keep nothing – except the purse.

PERCY: Perfidious villains!

SAIB: You mistake us, Sir; – we cannot be villains, for I, you know, am your Lordship's 'worthy friend!'

MULEY: And I your Lordship's unworthy pensioner!

PERCY: Confusion! – To be made the jest of such rascals!

SAIB: Earl Percy, we are none! – but we should have been, could your gold have bribed us to betray our master. We have but done our duty – you have but gained your just reward; for they who seek to deceive others, should ever be deceived themselves.

PERCY: Silence, fellow! – Leave me to my thoughts! – (Throwing himself passionately upon the couch.)

MULEY: Oh! with all our hearts! We ask no better.

SAIB: Muley, we share that purse?

MULEY: Undoubtedly: Sit down, and examine its contents – (They seat themselves on the floor in the front of the stage.)

PERCY: How unfortunate, that the only merit of these villains should be fidelity! – No hope now is left! Angela is lost, and with her my happiness!

CHORUS OF VOICES (Singing without.)

'Sing Megen-oh! Oh! Megen-Ee!'

MULEY: Hark! – What's that?

SAIB: I'll see. (Mounting upon the table.) – This window is so high–

MULEY: Here, here! Take this chair. – (Saib places the chair upon the table, and thus lifts himself to a level with the window, which he opens.)–

MOTLEY: (Singing without.) Sleep you, or wake you, Lady bright?

SONG AND CHORUS.

MOTLEY: (Singing without.) Sleep you, or wake you, Lady bright?

CHORUS: (Without.) Sing Megen-oh! Oh! Megen-Ee!

MOTLEY: Now is the fittest time for flight.

CHORUS: Sing Megen-oh! Oh! Megen-Ee!

MOTLEY: Know, from your tyrant father's power

Beneath the window of your tower

A boat now waits to set you free:

CHORUS: Sing Megen-oh! Oh! Megen-Ee!

Sing Megen-oh! Oh! Megen-Ee!

PERCY: (Who has half-raised himself from the couch during the latter part of the Song, and listened attentively.) – Surely I know that voice!

MULEY: Now, what's the matter?

SAIB: A boat lies at the foot of the tower, and the fishermen sing while they draw their nets.

PERCY: I could not be mistaken:– it was Gilbert!

SAIB: Hark! They begin again!–

SECOND STANZA.

MOTLEY: Though deep the stream, though high the wall,

CHORUS: Sing Megen-oh! Oh! Megen-Ee!

MOTLEY: The danger, trust me, Love, is small:

CHORUS: Sing Megen-oh! Oh! Megen-Ee!

MOTLEY: To spring below then never dread;

My arms to catch you shall be spread;

And far from hence you soon shall be,

CHORUS: Sing Megen-oh! Oh! Megen-Ee!

Sing Megen-oh! Oh! Megen-Ee!

PERCY: I understand him! He bids me – Yet the danger – What course shall I pursue?

MULEY: Pr'ythee, come down, Saib; I long to divide the purse–

SAIB: Stay a moment: one more stanza, and I'm with you. Now, silence!

THIRD STANZA.

MOTLEY: Fair Emma hushed her heart's alarms:

CHORUS: Sing Megen-oh! Oh! Megen-Ee!

MOTLEY: She sprang into her Lover's arms;

CHORUS: Sing Megen-oh! Oh! Megen-Ee!

MOTLEY: Unhurt she fell; then swift its way

The boat pursued without delay,

While Emma placed on Edgar's knee

Sang 'Megen-oh! Oh! Megen-Ee!'

CHORUS: Sing Megen-oh! Oh! Megen-Ee!

MULEY: Will you never quit that window?

SAIB: (Shutting it, and descending.) Here I am, and now for the purse – (They resume their seats upon the ground; Saib opens the purse, and begins to reckon the gold.)

PERCY: Yes, I must brave the danger – I will feign to sleep; and when my gaolers are off their guard, then aid me, blest Providence! – (Extending himself upon the couch.)

SAIB: Hold, Muley! – What if, instead of sharing the purse, we throw for its contents? Here are dice.

MULEY: With all my heart:– And look! to pass our time better, here's a bottle of the best sack in the Earl's cellar.

SAIB: Good! Good! – And now, be this angel for stake! – But, first, what is our prisoner doing?

MULEY: Oh! He sleeps: Mind him not. – Come, come – Throw!

SAIB: Here goes – Nine! – Now to you.

MULEY: Nine too! – Double the stake.

SAIB: Agreed! and the throw is mine. – Hark! What noise? – (During this dialogue, Percy has approached the table in silence; at the moment that he prepares to mount it, Saib looks round, and Percy hastily throws himself back upon the couch.)

MULEY: Oh! – Nothing, nothing!

SAIB: Methought I heard the Earl–

MULEY: Mere fancy! – You see he is sleeping soundly. Come, come – Throw!

SAIB: There then – Eleven!

MULEY: That's bad – Huzza! – Sixes!

SAIB: Plague on your fortune! – Come, Double or quits!

MULEY: Be it so, and I throw. – Zounds! Only Five!

SAIB: Then I think this hit must be mine. – Aces, by heavens!

MULEY: Ha! Ha! Ha! Your health, friend!

PERCY: (Who has again reached the table, mounted the chair, and, opening the window, now stands at it, and signs to the men below.) – They see me, and extend a cloth beneath the window! – 'Tis a fearful height!

SAIB: Do you mean to empty the bottle! – Come, come – Give it me.

MULEY: Take it, blunder-head! – (Saib drinks.)

PERCY: They encourage me to venture! – Now then, or never! – (Aloud.) Angels of bliss, protect me! – (He throws himself from the window.)[3]

MULEY AND SAIB: (Starting at the noise.) – Hell and Furies!

SAIB: (Dashes down the bottle, and climbs to the window hastily, while Muley remains below in an attitude of surprise.) – Escaped! Escaped!

PERCY, MOTLEY, &C. (Without.) – Huzza! huzza! huzza!

END OF THE SECOND ACT

---

[3] This incident has been cried out against by many people, as being improbable; and some have gone so far as to term it impossible. To this I can only answer, with Alice in the First Act – 'I never said it was possible, I only say it's true!' – This incident was furnished me by the German History, in which it appears, that a certain Landgrave of Thuringia, being condemned to death, made his escape by taking so desperate a leap from a window of his prison, that he was afterwards known throughout Germany by the name of 'Ludwig the Springer.' – There is a German Play on this subject, whence I borrowed the idea of making the gaolers play at dice; and Motley's Song bears some resemblance to an incident in Richard Coeur-de-Lion.

ACT III

SCENE I. – A View of the River Conway, with a Fisherman's Hut. – sunset.

Enter Allan and Edric.

ALLAN: Still they come not! – Dear, dear, still they come not! – Ah! these tumults are too much for my old body to bear.

EDRIC: Then you should have kept your old body at home. 'Tis a fine thing truly for a man of your age to be galloping about the country after a girl, who, by your own account, is neither your chick nor child!

ALLAN: Ah! She was more to me! She was my all, Edric, my all! – How could I bear my home when it no longer was the home of Angela? How could I rest in my cottage at night when her sweet lips had not kissed me – and murmured, 'Father, sleep well!' – She is so good! so gentle! – I was sick once, sick almost to death! Angela was then my nurse and comforter: She watched me when I slept, and cheered me when I woke: She rejoiced when I grew better; and when I grew worse, no medicine gave me ease like the tears of pity which fell on my burning cheeks from the eyes of my darling!

EDRIC: Tears of pity indeed! A little rhubarb would have done you more good by half. – But our people stay a long time: Perhaps Motley has been discovered and seized; if so, he will lose his life, the Earl his freedom, Angela her lover, and, what's worst of all, I shall lose my boat! I wish I hadn't lent it, for I doubt that Motley's scheme has failed.

ALLAN: I hope not – Oh! I hope not! – Should Percy remain a captive, Angela will be left unprotected in your wicked Lord's power – Oh! that will break my poor old wife's heart for certain!

EDRIC: And if it should break it, a mighty misfortune truly! – Zounds, Master Allan, any wife is at best a bad thing: a poor one makes matters get worse; but when she's old, Lord! 'tis the very devil!

ALLAN: Hark! Hark! Do you hear? – 'Tis the sound of oars! – They are our friends! – Oh! Heaven be thanked! the Earl is with them.

A boat appears with Percy, Motley, and soldiers disguised as fishermen. They land.

PERCY: (Springing on shore.) – Once more then I breathe the air of liberty! – Worthy Gilbert, what words can suffice to thank you?

MOTLEY. None – therefore do not waste your breath in the attempt. You are safe, thanks to St. Peter and the Blanket! and your Lady's deliverance now demands all your thoughts. – Ha! who is that with Edric?

PERCY: Allan, by all my hopes! – Welcome, welcome, good old man! – Say, came my vassals with you?

ALLAN: Three hundred chosen men are within the sound of your bugle. They scarce gave me time to signify your orders ere they sat in their saddles; and as I would needs come with them, Heaven forgive them for it! they put me on an hard-trotting horse! – Marry, he shook me rarely! he has almost broken my old bones:– But that matters little; my heart would have been broken had I staid behind. – But now, My Lord, tell me of Angela. Is she well? Did you speak to her? and speaks she sometimes of me?

PERCY: She is well, my old friend, and I have spoken to her – though but for a moment. Scarce had I time to confess to her my rank, when Kenric, whose suspicious eye had penetrated my disguise, forced me from her presence. But be comforted, good Allan! Should other means fail, I will this very night attack the Castle, and compel Osmond to resign his prey.

ALLAN: Heaven grant that you may succeed! – Let me but once see Angela your bride! Let me but once hear her say the sweet words, 'Allan, I am happy!' then I and my old wife will seek our graves, lay us down, and die with pleasure!

MOTL: Die with pleasure, you silly old man! you shall do nothing so ridiculous: You shall live a great many years; and, instead of lying down in your grave, we'll tuck you up warm with your old wife in the best down-bed of Alnwic Castle. – But now let us talk of our affairs, which, if I mistake not, are in the high road to success.

PERCY: How? Has any intelligence reached you of your ally, the Friar?

MOTL: You have guessed it. As it passed beneath his window, the pious porpus contrived to drop this letter into the boat. Its contents must needs be of consequence; for I assure you it comes from one of the greatest men in England. Pray examine it, my Lord! I never can read when the wind's easterly.

PERCY: I believe, Gilbert, were it northerly you would be no jot the wiser: I remember that many a sound stick did our preceptor break upon your back in vain; and before you had learned to spell, your schooling had cost my father a forest.

MOTL: (While Percy reads.) Nay, if learning could have been beaten into me, by this time I should be a prodigious scholar! – To do him justice, Father Benjamin had a most instructive jirk with his arm, and frequently used arguments so forcible when pointing out my faults, that many a time and oft has he brought tears into my eyes: Then I generally felt so penitent, and so low, that I was obliged to steal his brandy-bottle in order to recover my spirits. – Well, Sir, what says the letter?

PERCY: Listen. – 'I have recognised you in spite of your disguise, and seize the opportunity to advise your exerting yourself solely to obtain Earl Percy's liberty. Heed not Angela: I have sure and easy means for procuring her escape; and before the clock strikes two, you may expect me with her at the fisherman's hut. Farewell, and rely upon Father Philip.' – Now, Gilbert, what say you? May the monk's fidelity be trusted?

MOTL: His fidelity may undoubtedly; but whether his success will equal his good intentions is a point which time alone can decide. Should it not–

PERCY: Then with my faithful vassals will I storm the Castle tomorrow.

ALLAN: What, storm the Castle! – Oh! no, no! My darling never saw a bird die but she wept; then how will she bear to look on when men perish?

PERCY: Be assured, old man, that nothing save invincible necessity shall induce me to bathe my hands in the blood of my fellow-creatures. – But where are my followers.

ALLAN: Fearing lest their numbers should excite suspicion, I left them concealed in yonder wood.

PERCY: Guide me to them. Edric, for this night I must request the shelter of your hut.

EDRIC: Willingly, my Lord! But my cottage is so humble, your treatment so wretched–

PERCY: Silence, my good fellow! The hut, where good-will resides, is to me more welcome than a palace, and no food can be so sweet as that which is seasoned with smiles-You give me your best; a monarch could give no more, and it happens not often that men ever give so much. Now farewell for an hour-Allan, lead on! (Exeunt Percy, Allan, &C.)

Manent Motley and Edric.

MOTL: And in the meanwhile, friend Edric, I'll lend you an hand in preparing supper.

EDRIC: Truly the task won't give you much trouble, for times have gone hard with me of late. Our present Lord sees no company, gives no entertainments, and thus I sell no fish. Things went better while Earl Reginald lived!

MOTL: What! you remember him!

EDRIC: Never shall I forget him, or his sweet Lady! Why, I verily believe, they possessed all the cardinal virtues! – So pious, so generous, so mild! so kind to the poor, and so fond of fish!

MOTL: Fond of fish! – One of the cardinal virtues, of which I never heard before!

EDRIC: But these thoughts make me sad. Come, Master Motley; your Lord's supper still swims in the river:– if you'll help to catch it, why do so, and thank you heartily. Can you fish?

MOTL: Can I! Who in this world cannot? – I'll assure you, friend Edric, there is no profession more universal than yours; we all spread our nets to catch something or other – and alas! when obtained, it seldom proves worth the trouble of taking. The Coquette fishes for hearts which are worthless; the Courtier, for titles which are absurd;[4] and the Poet, for compliments which are empty. – Oh! happy are they in this world of disappointments, who throw out no nets save fishing ones. (Exeunt)

---

[4] On the strength of this single sentence, it was boldly asserted on the morning after the first performance, that the whole Play was written to support the Cause of Equality; and that I said in it, all distinctions of rank ought to be abolished, and thought it extremely wrong for any persons to accept titles! To make the thing complete, the assertors should have added, that I thought it extremely wrong for any persons to pay compliments, or possess hearts!

***

SCENE II. – The Castle-Hall.

Enter Kenric.

KENR: Yonder he stalks, and seems buried in himself! – Now then to attack him while my late service is still fresh upon his memory. Should he reject my petition positively, he shall have good cause to repent his ingratitude. Percy is in the neighbourhood; and that secret, known only to myself, will surely – But, silence! – Look where he comes!

Enter Osmond.

OSM: It shall not be! Away with these foreboding terrors, which weigh down my heart! – Does not all smile upon my fortunes? My rival wears my chains; he cannot wrest her from me, and with tomorrow's dawn Angela shall be mine. Bound then high, my heart! Pleasure, sweet guest, so long a stranger, Oh! to my bosom welcome once more! – I will forget the past, I will enjoy the present, and make those raptures again mine, which – Ah! no, no, no! – Conscience, that serpent, winds her folds round the cup of my bliss, and, ere my lips can reach it, her venom is mingled with the draught.

KENR: How profound the gloom which obscures his brow! – How fixed, how hopeless glares his dark eyeball! – Oh! dreadful is the villain's look, when he ponders on committed crimes!

OSM: Evening approaches fast – (Drawing near and opening the window.) Already the air breathes cooler, and the beams of the setting sun sparkle on the waters of Conway. How fair, how tranquil all without! How dark, how comfortless all within! – Hark! the sound of music! – The peasants are returning from labour: they move with gay and careless steps, carolling as they go some rustic ditty; and will pass the night in rest, for they have passed the day in innocence!

CHORUS (Without.)

Pleased the toils of day to leave,

Home we haste with foot-steps light:

Oh! how gay the cotter's eve!

Oh! how calm the cotter's night!

OSM: (Closing the window with violence.) – Curses upon them – I will look, I will listen no more! I sicken at the sight of happiness, which I never more must enjoy; I hate the possessors of hearts untainted – hate, for I envy! – Oh! fly from my eyes, bright Day! Speed thy pace, Darkness! thou art my love! Haste to unfold thy sable mantle, and robe the world in the colour of my soul!

KENR: Now then to accost him – Yet I tremble!

OSM: Anguish! endless, hopeless anguish! – Day or night, no moment of rest – When I sleep, dreams of strange horror still fright me from my couch! When I wake, I find in every object some cause for distrust – read the dread charge in every eye, 'Thou art a murderer!' – and tremble lest the agents of my guilt should work its punishment. – And see where he walks, the chief object of my fears! – He shall not be so long! – His anxiety to leave me, his later mysterious threats – No, no! I will not live in fear. – Soft! – he advances!

KENR: So melancholy, my Lord?

OSM: Aye, Kenric, and must be so, till Angela is mine. Know that even now she extorted from me a promise, that till tomorrow I would leave her unmolested.

KENR: But till tomorrow?

OSM: But till tomorrow? – Oh! in that little space a lover's eye views myriads of dangers! – Yet think not, good Kenric, that your late services are undervalued by me, or that I have forgotten those for which I have been long your debtor. When, bewildered by hatred of Reginald, and grief for Evelina's loss, my dagger was placed on the throat of their infant, your hand arrested the blow – Judge then how grateful I must feel when I behold in Angela her mother's living counterpart – behold her such as when, shielding with her body her fallen husband, Evelina received that dagger in her breast which I aimed at the heart of Reginald! – Worthy Kenric, how can I repay your services!

KENR: These you may easily. – But what, Earl Osmond, what can repay me for the sacrifice of my innocence? – I was virtuous till you bade me be guilty – my hands were pure till you taught me to stain them with blood – you painted in strong colours the shame of servitude – you promised freedom, riches, independence – you vanquished the resistance of my better

Angel, and never since have I known one moment of rest!

OSM: Good Kenric–

KFNR. All here reminds me of my guilt – every object recalls to me Reginald and his murdered Lady! – Let me then claim that independence so long promised, and seek for peace in some other climate, since memory forbids me to taste it in this.

OSM: Kenric, ere named, your wish was granted. In a far distant country a retreat is already prepared for you: there may you hush those clamours of conscience, which must reach me, I fear, e'en in the arms of Angela. Yet do not leave me till she is my bride – Stay yet a week in Conway Castle; and then, though 'twill cost me many a pang, Kenric, you shall bid it a long adieu. – Are you contented?

KENR: (Affected.) My Lord! – Gratitude – Amazement – And I doubted – I suspected – Oh! my good Lord, how have I wronged your kindness!

OSM: No more – I must not hear you! – (Aside.) – Shame! shame! that ever my soul should stoop to dissembling with my slave! – Kenric, farewell! – Till Angela is mine, keep a strict eye on Percy; and then–

Saib enters, and advances with apprehension.

OSM: How now? – Why this confusion? – Why do you tremble? – Speak!

SAIB: My Lord! – the prisoner–

OSM: The prisoner? – Go on! go on!

SAIB: (Kneeling.) Pardon, my Lord, pardon! Our prisoner has escaped!

OSM: Villain! – (Wild with rage he draws his dagger, and rushes upon Saib – Kenric holds his arm.)

KENR: Hold! hold! – What would you do?

OSM: (Struggling.) Unhand me, or by Heaven–

KENR: Away! away! – Fly fellow, fly and save yourself (Exit Saib.)

KENR: (Releasing Osmond.) Consider, my Lord – haply 'twas not by his keeper's fault that–

OSM: (Furiously.) What is't to me by whose? – Is not my rival fled? – Soon will Northumberland's guards encircle my walls, and force from me – Yet that by Heaven they shall not! No! Rather then resign her, my own hand shall give this Castle a prey to flames: then plunging with Angela into the blazing gulph, I'll leave these ruins to tell posterity how desperate was my love, and how dreadful my revenge! – (Going, he stops, and turns to Kenric.) – And you, who dared to rush between me and my resentment – you who could so well succeed in saving others – now look to yourself (Exit)

KENR: Ha! that look – that threat – Yet he seemed so kind, so grateful! – He smiled too! – Oh! there is ever danger when a villain smiles.

(Saib enters softly, looking round him with caution.)

SAIB: (In a low voice.) Hist! – Kenric!

KENR: How now? – What brings–

SAIB: Silence, and hear me! – You have saved my life, nor will I be ungrateful – Look at this phial!

KENR: Ha! did the Earl–

SAIB: Even so: a few drops of this liquor should tonight have flavoured your wine – you would never have drank again! Mark me then – When I offer you a goblet at supper, drop it as by accident. For this night I give you life: use it to quit the Castle; for no longer than till to-morrow dare I disobey our Lord's commands. Farewell, and fly from Conway – You bear with you my thanks! (Exit)

KENR: Can it be possible? Is not all this a dream? – Villain! villain! – Yes, yes, I must away! – But tremble, traitor! – A bolt, of which you little think, hangs over, and shall crush you! – The keys are still in my possession – Angela shall be the partner of my flight. – My prisoner too – Yet hold! May not resentment – may not Reginald's sixteen years captivity – Oh! no! Angela shall be my advocate; and, grateful for her own, for her parent's life preserved, she can, she will obtain my pardon – Yet, should she fail, at least I shall drag down Osmond in my fall, and sweeten death's bitter cup with vengeance! (Exit)

***

SCENE III. – The Cedar-room, with folding Doors in the middle, and a large antique Bed; on one Side is the

Portrait of a Lady, on the other that of a Warrior armed. Both are at full length. – After a pause the Female Portrait slides back and Father Philip, after looking in, advances cautiously.

F. PHIL: (Closing the pannel.) Thus far I have proceeded without danger, though not without difficulty. Yon narrow passage is by no means calculated for persons of my habit of body. By my Holidame, I begin to suspect that the fool is in the right! I certainly am growing corpulent. – And now, how shall I employ myself – Sinner that I am, why did I forget the bottle of sack? – The time will pass tediously till Angela comes. – And, to complete the business, yonder is the haunted Oratory. What if the ghost should pop out on me? Blessed St. Bridget, there would be a tête-à-tête! – Yet this is a foolish fear:– 'Tis yet scarce eight o'clock, and your ghosts always keep late hours; yet I don't like the idea of our being such near neighbours. If Alice says true, the apparition just now lives next door to me; but the Lord forbid that we should ever be visiting acquaintance! – Would I had something to drive her out my head! A good book now, or a bottle of sack, St. Augustine, or a cold venison pasty, would be worth its weight in gold: but in the chambers of these young girls one finds nothing good either to read, drink, or eat. Now my last patroness, the Baroness O'Drench – Ah! to hear the catalogue of her crimes was quite a pleasure, for she always confessed them over a sirloin of beef, and, instead of telling a bead, swallowed a bumper! – Oh! she was a worthy soul! – But hark! – Angela comes.

OSM: (Without.) What, Alice! – Alice, I say!

F. PHIL: By St. David, tis the Earl! I'll away as fast as I can! – (Trying to open the door.) – I can't find the spring! – Lord forgive me my sins! – Where can I hide myself – Ha! the bed! – 'Tis the very thing. – (Throws himself into the bed, and conceals himself under the clothes.) – Heaven grant that it mayn't break down with me; for, Oh! what a fall would be there, my countrymen! – They come! – (The door is unlocked.)

(Enter Osmond, Angela, and Alice.)

OSM: (Entering.) You have heard my will, Lady. Till your hand is mine, you quit not this chamber.

ANG: If then it must be so, welcome my eternal prison! – Yet eternal it shall not be! – My hero, my guardian-angel is at liberty! Soon shall his horn make these hateful towers tremble, and your fetters be exchanged for the arms of Percy!

OSM: Beware, beware, Angela! – Dare not before me–

ANG: Before you! before the world! – Is my attachment a disgrace? No! 'tis my pride; for its object is deserving. Long ere I knew him, Percy's fame was dear to me. While I still believed him the peasant Edwy; often, in his hearing, have I dwelt upon Northumberland's praise, and chid him that he spoke of our Lord so coldly! Ah! little did I think that the man then seated beside me was he whom I envied for his power of doing good, whom I loved for exerting that power so largely! – Judge then, Earl Osmond, on my arrival here how strongly I must have felt the contrast! – What peasant names you his benefactor? What beggar has been comforted by your bounty? what sick man preserved by your care? – Your breast is unmoved by woe, your ear is deaf to complaint, your doors are barred against the poor and wretched. Not so are the gates of Alnwic Castle; they are open as their owner's heart.

ALICE: My hair stands on end to hear her!

OSM: Insulting girl! – This to my face?

ANG: Nay, never bend your brows! – Shall I tremble, because you frown? Shall my eye sink, because anger flashes from yours? – No! that would ill become the bride of Northumberland.

OSM: Amazement! – Can this be the gentle, timid Angela?

ANG: Wonder you that the worm should turn when you trample it so cruelly! – Oh! wonder no more: Ere he was torn from me, I clasped Percy to my breast, and my heart caught a spark of that fire which flames in his unceasingly!

ALICE: Caught fire, Lady! – Bless me, I hope you didn't burn yourself?

OSM: Silence, old crone! – I have heard you calmly, Angela; now then hear me. Twelve hours shall be allowed you to reflect upon your situation: till that period is elapsed, this chamber shall be your prison, and Alice, on whose fidelity I can depend, your sole attendant. This term expired, should you still reject my hand, force shall obtain for me what love denies. Speak not: I will hear nothing! – I swear that tomorrow sees you mine, or undone! and, Skies, rain curses on me if I keep not my oath! – Mark that, proud girl! mark it, and tremble! (Exit)

F. PHIL: Heaven be praised, he's gone!

ANG: Tremble, did he say? – Alas! how quickly is my boasted courage vanished! – Yet I will not despair: there is a Power in heaven, there is a Percy on earth; on them will I rely to save me.

ALICE: The first may, Lady; but as to the second, he'll be of no use, depend on't. Now, might I advise, you'd accept my Lord's offer: What matters it whether the man's name be Osmond or Percy? An Earl's an Earl after all; and though one may be something richer than t'other–

ANG: Oh! silence, Alice! – nor aid my tyrant's designs: rather instruct me how to counteract them. You have influence in the Castle; assist me to escape, and be assured that Percy's gratitude and generosity–

ALICE: I help you to escape! Not for the best gown in your Ladyship's wardrobe! I tremble at the very idea of my Lord's rage; and, besides, had I the will, I've not the power. Kenric keeps the keys; we could not possibly quit the Castle without his knowledge; and if the Earl threatens to use force with you – Oh Gemini! what would he use with me, Lady?

ANG: Threatens, Alice! – I despise his threats! Ere it pillows Osmond's head will I plunge this poniard in my bosom.

ALICE: Holy fathers! – A dagger!

ANG: Even now, as I wandered through the Armoury, my eye was attracted by its glittering handle. – Look, Alice! it bears Osmond's name; and the point–

ALICE: Is rusty with blood! – Take it away, Lady! – Take it away! – I never see blood without fainting!

ANG: (Putting up the dagger.) This weapon may render me good service. – But, ah! what service has it rendered Osmond! – Haply 'twas this very poniard which drank his brother's blood – or which pierced the fair breast of Evelina! – Said you not, Alice, that this was her portrait?

ALICE: I did, Lady; and the likeness was counted excellent.

ANG: How fair! – How heavenly! – What sweetness, yet what dignity, in her blue, speaking eyes!

ALICE: No wonder that you admire her, Lady; she was as like you as one pea to another. But this morning you know I promised to show you her Oratory, and here I've brought the key. – Shall I unlock the door?

ANG: Do so, good Alice! – Haply for a moment it may abstract my thoughts from my own sorrows.

F. PHIL: (While Alice unlocks the door.) Will the old woman never be gone? – I dare not discover myself in her presence.

ALICE: (Having opened the folding doors, an Oratory is seen, richly ornamented with carving and painted glass:

Angela and Alice enter it.) This room has not been opened since my Lady's death, and every thing remains as she left it. Look, here is her veil – her prayer-book too, in which she was reading on the very night before she quitted the Castle, never to return!

F. PHIL: I'm out of all patience.

ALICE: And that guitar! – How often have I heard her play upon that guitar! She would sit in yonder window for hours, and still she played airs so sad, so sweet – To be sure, she had the finest voice that ever – (During this speech Angela, who at first looks round with curiosity, throws the veil carelessly over her face, and, taking the guitar from the table, strikes a few wild and melancholy notes. Alice, whose back is towards her, turns hastily round, screams, and rushes from the Oratory. Angela casts the veil and guitar upon the table, and follows her.)

ANG: What alarms you?

ALICE: Is it you, Lady? Let me die, if I didn't take you for the ghost! – Your air, your look, your attitude, all were so like the deceased Countess, that – Well, well! I'll not enter that room again in an hurry! I protest, my hand trembles so, that I can hardly turn the key!

ANG: How contagious is terror! This silly woman's apprehensions have spread to my bosom, and scarce can I look round without alarm. The stillness too of evening – The wavering and mysterious light which streams through these painted windows – And, hark! 'Twas the shriek of the screech-owl, which nests in the tower above!

ALICE: (Having locked the folding doors.) Ah! 'twas a sad day for me, when I heard of the dear Lady's loss! Look at that bed, Lady:– That very bed was hers.

F. PHIL: Was it so? Oh! ho!

ALICE: How often have I seen her sleeping in that bed – and, oh! How like an angel she looked when sleeping! I remember, that just after Earl Reginald – Oh! Lord! didn't somebody shake the curtain?

ANG: Absurd! It was the wind.

AI.ICE. I declare it made me tremble! Well, as I was saying, I remember, just after Earl Reginald had set out for the Scottish wars, going into her room one morning, and hearing her sob most bitterly. – So advancing to the bedside, as it might be thus – 'My Lady!' says I, with a low curtsey, 'Isn't your Ladyship well!' – So, with that, she raised her head slowly above the quilt, and, giving me a mournful look – (Here, unseen by Angela, who is contemplating Reginald's portrait, Father Philip lifts up his head, and gives a deep groan.)

ALICE: Jesu Maria! the devil! the devil! the devil![5]

ANG: (Turning round.) How now? (Father Philip rising from the bed – it breaks under him, and he rolls at Angela's feet.) – Good heavens! a man concealed! – (Attempting to pass him, he detains her by her robe.)

---

[5] This incident is borrowed form "The Mysteries of Udolpho", but employed very differently. In the Romance it brings forward a terrific scene. In the Play it is intended to produce an effect entirely ludicrous.

F. PHIL: Stay, daughter, stay! If you run, I can never overtake you!

ANG: Amazement! Father Philip!

F. PHIL: The very same, and at present the best friend that you have in the world. Daughter, I came to save you.

ANG: To save me? Speak! Proceed!

F. PHIL: Observe this picture; it conceals a spring, whose secret is unknown to all in the Castle except myself. Upon touching it, the pannel slides back, and a winding passage opens into the marble hall. Thence we must proceed to the vaulted vestibule; a door is there concealed, similar to this; and, after threading the mazes of a subterranean labyrinth, we shall find ourselves in safety on the outside of the Castle-walls.

ANG: Oh! worthy, worthy Father! quick let us hasten! Let us not not lose one moment!

F. PHIL: Hold! hold! Not so fast. You forget, that between the hall and vestibule we must traverse many chambers much frequented at this early hour. Wait till the Castle's inhabitants are asleep. Expect me, without fail, at one; keep up your spirits, and doubt not of success. Now then I must away, lest the Earl should perceive my absence.

ANG: Stay yet one moment. Tell me, does Percy–

F. PHIL: I have apprised him, that this night will restore you to liberty, and he expects you at the fisherman's cottage. Now, then, farewell, fair daughter!

ANG: Good Friar, till one, farewell!

(Exit F. Philip through the sliding pannel, closing it after him.)

ANG: This is thy doing, God of Justice! Receive my thanks. – Yes, Percy, we shall meet once more – shall meet never again to separate! Those dreams shall be realized – those smiling golden dreams which floated before us in Allan's happy cottage. Hand in hand shall we wander together through life – partners in pleasure – partners in woe – and when the night of our existence arrives, one spot shall receive our bodies – one stone shall cover our grave. – Allan too, and the worthy Maud! – my parents – my more than parents! – to smooth the pillow of their age – to gild their last hours with sun-shine! That thought is heaven. So glorious are my prospects, that they dazzle me to look on, and scarce can I believe them really to exist. – Oh! gracious God! should my brain be bewildered by fancy – should I be now the sport of some deceitful dream, seal up my eyes for ever, never let me wake again! – I must not expect the Friar before one. – Till that hour arrives, will I kneel at the feet of younder Saint, there tell my beads, and pray for morning!

END OF THE THIRD ACT

ACT IV

SCENE I. – The Castle-Hall: The Lamps are lighted.

Enter Father Philip.

F. PHIL: 'Tis near midnight, and the Earl is already retired to rest. What if I ventured now to the Lady's chamber? Hark! I hear the sound of footsteps!

Enter Alice.

F. PHIL: How, Alice, is it you?

ALICE: So! So! – Have I found you at last, Father? – I have been in search of you these four hours! – Oh! I've been so frightened since I saw you, that I wonder I keep my senses!

F. PHIL: So do I; for I'm sure they're not worth the trouble. And, pray, what has alarmed you thus? I warrant you've taken an old cloak pinned against the wall for a spectre, or discovered the devil in the shape of a tabby-cat.

ALICE: (Looking round in terror.) For the love of heaven, Father, don't name the devil! or, if you must speak of him, pray mention the good gentleman with proper politeness. I'm sure, for my own part, I had always a great respect for him, and if he hears me, I dare say he'll own as much.

F. PHIL: Respect for the devil, you wicked woman! – for that perfidious serpent – that crafty seducer–

ALICE: Hush! – Hush! – Father, you make my teeth chatter with fright. For aught I know he's within hearing, for he certainly haunts this Castle in the form of my late Lady.

F. PHIL: Form of a fiddlestick! – Don't tell me of your–

ALICE: Father, on the word of a virgin, I saw him this very evening in Lady Angela's bed!

F. PHIL: In Lady Angela's? – On my conscience, the devil has an excellent taste! But, Alice! – Alice! – how dare you trot about the house at this time of night, propagating such abominable falsehoods? – One comfort is, that nobody will believe you. Lady Angela's virtue is too well known, and I'm persuaded she wouldn't suffer the devil to put a single claw into her bed for the universe!

ALICE: How you run on! – Lord bless me, she wasn't in bed herself.

F. PHIL: Oh! – Was she not?

ALICE: No, to be sure: But you shall hear how it happened. We were in the Cedar-room together; and while we were talking of this and that, Lady Angela suddenly gave a great scream. I looked round, and what should I see but a tall figure all in white extended upon the bed! At the same time I heard a voice, which I knew to be the Countess Evelina's, pronounce in a hollow tone – 'Alice! – Alice! – Alice!' – three times. You may be certain that I was frightened enough. I instantly took to my heels; and just as I got without side of the door, I heard a loud clap of thunder, and the whole chamber shook as if tumbling into a thousand pieces!

F. PHIL: Well done, Alice! – A very good story, upon my word: It has but one fault – 'Tis not true.

ALICE: Ods my life, Father, how can you tell any thing about it? Sure I should know best; for I was there, and you were not. I repeat it – I heard the voice as plain as I hear yours: Do you think I've no ears?

F. PIIIL. Oh! far from it: I think you've uncommonly good ones; for you not only hear what has been said, but what has not. Hark! – the clock strikes twelve:– 'Tis late, and I'm sleepy, so shall bid you farewell for the present. As to this wonderful story of yours, Alice, I don't believe one word of it: I'll be sworn that the voice was no more like your Lady's than like mine; and that the devil was no more in the bed than I was. Therefore, take my advice, set your heart at rest, and go quietly to your chamber, as I am now going to mine. – Goodnight.

ALICE: Goodnight? – Surely you'll not have the heart to leave me in this terrible situation! – Suppose Satan should appear to me when I'm alone! – Sinner that I am, I should certainly die of the fright! – Good Father, you are a priest, and an holy man; your habit frightens the evil spirits, and they dare not come near you:– Oh! if you will but suffer me to pass the night in your company–

F. PHIL: Oh! monstrous! – Oh! impudence unparalleled! – You naughty, naughty woman, what could put such thoughts in your head?

ALICE: What's the matter now?

F. PHIL: Does not my sacred habit inspire you with awe? – Does not the exemplary chastity of my past life warn you to conceal such licentious desires? – Pass the night with me indeed? – I'm shocked at the very thought!

ALICE: The man's mad! – Father, as I hope to be saved–

F. PHIL: Nay! – Come not near me! – Offer not to embrace me!

ALICE: I embrace you! – Lord! Fellow, I wouldn't touch you for the universe.

F. PHIL: Was it for this that you still flattered my person, and declared that nothing became a man more than a big belly? – Was it for this that you strove to win my heart through the medium of my stomach; that you used to come languishing every day with some liquorish dish; and, while you squeezed my left hand tenderly, placed a sack-posset in the right? – Heavens! how deep-laid were your plans of seduction! – But mark me, tempter: In vain has the soup been salted, the ragout seasoned, and the pepperbox shaken with unsparing hand! My virtue is proof against all your culinary spells; the fairness of my innocence is still unblemished; and in spite of your luscious stews and savoury hashes, I retire like a second St. Anthony, victorious front Temptation's lists! (Exit.)

ALICE: There, he's gone! – Dear heart! Dear heart! what shall I do now? – 'Tis past twelve o'clock, and stay by myself I dare not. – I'll e'en wake the laundry-maid, make her sit up in my room all night; and 'tis hard if two women a'n't a match for the best devil in Christendom. (Exit)

Enter Saib and Hassan.

SAIB: The Earl then has forgiven me! – A moment longer, and his pardon would have come too late. Had not Kenric held his hand, by this time I should be at supper with St. Peter.

HASS: Your folly well deserved such a reward. Knowing the Earl's hasty nature, you should have shunned him till the first storm of passion was past, and circumstances had again made your ministry needful. Anger then would have armed his hand in vain; for interest, the white-man's God, would have blunted the point of his dagger.

SAIB: I trusted that his gratitude for my past services–

HASS: European gratitude? – Seek constancy in the winds – fire in ice – darkness in the blaze of sunshine! – But seek not gratitude in the breast of an European!

SAIB: Then, why so attached to Osmond? For what do you value him?

HASS: Not for his virtues, but for his vices, Saib: Can there for me be a great cause to love him? – Am I not branded with scorn? Am I not marked out for dishonour? Was I not free, and am I not a slave? Was I not once beloved, and am I not now despised? What man, did I tender my service, would accept the negro's friendship? What woman, did I talk of affection, would not turn from the negro with disgust? Yet, in my own dear land, my friendship was courted, my love was returned. I had parents, children, wife! – Bitter thought, in one moment all were lost to me! Can I remember this, and not hate these white men? Can I think how cruelly they have wronged me, and not rejoice when I see them suffer? – Attached to Osmond, say you? Saib, I hate him! Yet viewing him as an avenging Fiend sent hither to torment his fellows, it glads me that he fills his office so well! Oh! 'tis a thought which I would not barter for empires, to know that in this world he makes others suffer, and will suffer himself for their tortures in the next!

SAIB: But say, you be one of those whom he causes to suffer, how then? Hassan, I will sleep no more in the Lion's den! My resolve is taken: I will away from the Castle, and seek in some other service that security–

OSM: (Within) – What – Hoa! Help! – Lights there! Lights!

HASS: Hark! Surely 'twas the Earl!

(Osmond rushes in wildly.)

OSM: Save me! Save me! – They are at hand! Oh! let them not enter! – (Sinks into the arms of Saib.)

SAIB: What call this mean? – See how his eyes roll! How violently he trembles!

HASS: Speak, my Lord! – Do you not know us?

OSM: (Recovering himself.) Ha! Whose voice? – Hassan's – And Saib too here? – Oh! Was it then but a dream? – Did I not hear those dreadful, those damning words? –

Still, still they ring in my ears. Hassan! Hassan! Death must be bliss, in flames or on the rack, compared to what I have this night suffered!

HASS: Compose yourself, my Lord: Can a mere dream unman you thus?

OSM: A mere dream, say'st thou? Hassan, 'twas a dream of such horror! Did such dreams haunt my bitterest foe, I should wish him no severer punishment. Mark you not, how the ague of fear still makes my limbs tremble? Rolls not my eye, as if still gazing on the Spectre? Are not my lips convulsed, as were they yet prest by the kiss of corruption? Oh! 'twas a sight, that might have bleached joy's rosy cheek for ever, and strowed the snows of age upon youth's auburn ringlets! Yet, away with these terrors! – Hassan, thou saidst, 'twas but a dream: I was deceived by fancy. Hassan, thou saidst true; there is not, there cannot be, a world to come.

HASS: My Lord!–

OSM: Answer me not! Let me not hear the damning truth! Tell me not, that flames await me! that for moments of bliss I must endure long ages of torture! Plunge me rather in the thickest gloom of Atheism! Say, that with my body must perish my soul! For, oh! should my fearful dream be prophetic! Hark, fellows! Instruments of my guilt, listen to my punishment! – Methought I wandered through the low-browed caverns, where repose the reliques of my ancestors! My eye dwelt with awe on their tombs, with disgust on Mortality's surrounding emblems! Suddenly a female form glided along the vault: It was Angela! She smiled upon me, and beckoned me to advance. I flew towards her; my arms were already unclosed to clasp her – when suddenly her figure changed, her face grew pale, a stream of blood gushed from her bosom! – Hassan, 'twas Evelina!

SAIB AND HASS: Evelina!

OSM: Such as when she sank at my feet expiring, while my hand grasped the dagger still crimsoned with her blood! – 'We meet again this night!' murmured her hollow voice! 'Now rush to my arms, but first see what you have made me! Embrace me, my bridegroom! We must never part again!' – While speaking, her form withered away: the flesh fell from her bones; her eyes burst from their sockets: a skeleton, loathsome and meagre, clasped me in her mouldering arms!–

SAIB: Most horrible!

OSM: Her infected breath was mingled with mine; her rotting fingers pressed my hand, and my face was covered with her kisses! Oh! then, then how I trembled with disgust! And now blue dismal flames gleamed along the walls; the tombs were rent asunder; bands of fierce spectres rushed round me in frantic dance! furiously they gnashed their teeth while they gazed upon me, and shrieked in loud yell – 'Welcome, thou fratricide! Welcome, thou lost for ever!' – Horror burst the bands of sleep; distracted I flew hither: But my feelings – words are too weak, too powerless to express them.

SAIB: My Lord, my Lord, this was no idle dream! 'Twas a celestial warning; – 'twas your better Angel that whispered – 'Osmond, repent your former crimes! Commit not new ones!' – Remember, that this night should Kenric–

OSM: Kenric? – Oh! speak! Drank he the poison?

SAIB: Obedient to your orders, I presented it at supper; but ere the cup reached his lips, his favorite dog sprang upon his arm, and the liquor fell to the ground untasted.

OSM: Praised be Heaven! Then my soul is lighter by a crime! – Kenric shall live, good Saib. What though he quit me, and betray my secrets? Proofs he cannot bring against me, and bare assertions will not be believed. At worst, should his tale be credited, long ere Percy can wrest her from me, shall Angela be mine. Angela! – Oh! At that name all again is calm in my bosom. Hushed by her image my tumultuous passions sink to rest, and my terrors subside into that single fear, her loss! I forget that I have waded to her arms through blood; forget all save my affection and her beauty!

SAIB: You forget too that her heart is another's? Oh! my Lord, reflect on your conduct while it is yet time; restore the poor Angela to liberty; resign her to her favourite lover–

OSM: Sooner will I resign my life! – Fellow, you know not what you say: My heartstrings are twisted round the maid; ere I resign her, those strings must break. If I exist tomorrow night, I will pass it in her arms – If I exist? – Ha! Whence the doubt? 'We meet again this night!' – So said the Spectre! – Dreadful words, be ye blotted from my mind for ever. – Hassan, to your vigilance I leave the care of my beloved. Fly to me that instant, should any unbidden footstep approach yon chamber-door. I'll to my couch again. Follow me, Saib, and watch me while I sleep. Then, if you see my limbs convulsed, my teeth clenched, my hair bristiling, and cold dews trembling on my brow, seize me! Rouse me! Snatch me from my bed! I must not dream again. – Oh! faithless Sleep, why art thou too leagued with my foes? There was a time when thy presence brought oblivion to my sorrows; when thy poppy-crown was mingled with roses! – Now, Fear and Remorse thy sad companions, I shudder to see thee approach my couch! Blood trickles from thy garments; snakes writhe around thy brows: thy hand holds the well-known fatal dagger, and plunges it still reeking in my breast! – Then do I shriek in agony; then do I start distracted from thy arms! – Oh! how I hate thee, Sleep! – Friend of Virtue, oh! how I dread thy coming![6]

(Exit with Saib.)

HASS: (Alone.) – Yes, thou art sweet, Vengeance! – Oh! how it joys me when the white man suffers! Yet weak are his pangs, compared to those I felt when torn from thy shores, O native Africa! from thy bosom, my faithful Samba! – Ah! dost thou still exist, my wife? Has sorrow for my loss traced thy smooth brow with wrinkles! – My boy too, whom on that morning when the man-hunters seized me, I left sleeping on thy bosom, say, Lives he yet? Does he ever speak of me? Does he ask, 'Mother, describe to me my father; show me how the warrior

---

[6] This scene will doubtless have reminded the Reader of Clarence's Dream, Richard's Dream, &c.: But it bears a much closer resemblance to the Dream of Francis in Schiller's Robbers, which, in my opinion, is surpassed by no vision ever related upon the Stage. Were I asked to produce an instance of the terrific and sublime, I should name the Parricide's confession – Ich kannte den Mann!

looked?'[7] has my bosom still room for thoughts so tender? Hence with them! Vengeance must possess it all! Oh! when I forget my wrongs, may I forget myself! When I forbear to hate these Christians, God of my fathers! mayst thou hate me! – Ha! Whence that light? A man moves this way with a lamp! How cautiously he steals along! He must be watched. This friendly column will shield me from his regards. Silence! he comes. (Retires.)

Kenric enters softly with a Lamp.

KENR: All is hushed! – The Castle seems buried in sleep. – Now then to Angela! (Exit.)

HASS: (Advancing.) – It was Kenrick – Still he moves onwards – Now he stops – 'T'is at the door of Angela's chamber! – He unlocks it! – He enters! – Away then to the Earl: Christian, soon shall we meet again!

(Exit)

**

SCENE II. – Angela's apartment.

Angela stands by the Window, which is open, and through which the Moon is seen.

ANGELA. Will it never arrive, this tedious lingering hour? Sure an age must have elapsed since the Friar left me, and still the bell strikes not one! – Percy, does thy impa-

---

[7] I suspect this last idea to be the property of some other person, but what other person I know not: It is much at the service of any one who may think it worth claiming.

tience equal mine? Dost thou too count the moments which divide us? Dost thou too chide the slowness of Time's pinions, which moved so swiftly when we strayed together on the Cheviot Hills? – Methinks I see him now, as he paces the Conway's margin: If a leaf falls, if a bird flutters, he flies towards it, for he thinks 'tis the footstep of Angela: Then, with slow steps and bending head, disappointed he regains the fisher's cottage. Perhaps, at this moment, his eyes like mine are fixed on yonder planet; perhaps, this sweet wind which plays on my cheek, is freighted with the sighs of my Lover. – Oh! sigh no more, my Percy! Soon shall I repose in safety on your bosom; soon again see the moon shed her silver light on Cheviot, and hear its green hills repeat the carol of your mellow horn!

SONG

How slow the lingering moments wear!
Ye hours, in pity speed your flight,
Till Cheviot's hills so fresh and fair
Again shall meet my longing sight!
Oh! then what rapture 'twill afford
Once more those scenes beloved to see,
Where Percy's heart first told its Lord,
He loved the Lass of lowdegree![8]

No founding titles graced my name,
No bounteous kinsmen swelled my dower;
But Percy sought no highborn Dame,
But Percy sought not wealth or power.
He sought a fond, a faithful heart,

---

[8] Owing to the great exertions which her character demanded, Mrs. Jordan omitted this Song.

He found the heart he sought in me;
He saw her pure and free from art,
And loved the Lass of low degree.

The Castle seems to be still already: Would the Friar had named an earlier hour! By this I might have been safe in the fisher's cottage – Hark! Surely I heard – Some one unlocks the door! – Oh! should it be the Earl! Should he not retire ere the Monk arrives! – The door opens! – How! – Kenric here! – Speak – What would you?

Enter Kenric.

KENR: Softly, Lady! – If overheard, I am lost, and your fate is connected with mine – (Placing his lamp on the table.)

ANG: What means this mystery? – This midnight visit–

KENR: Is the visit of a Friend, of a Penitent! – Lady, I must away from the Castle: The keys are in my possession: I will make you the companion of my flight, and deliver you safe into the hands of Percy. – But, ere we depart – (Kneeling) – Oh! tell me, Lady, will you plead for me with one, who to me alone owes sixteen years of hard captivity?

ANG: Rise, Kenric: I understand you not. Of what captive do you speak?

KENR: Of one, who by me has been most injured, who to you will be most dear. Listen, Lady, to my strange narration. I was brought up with Osmond, was the partner of his pleasures, the confident of his cares. The latter sprang solely from his elder brother, whose birthright he coveted, whose superiority he envied. Yet his aversion burst not forth, till Evelina Neville, rejecting his hand, bestowed hers with her heart on Reginald. Then did Osmond's passion over-leap all bounds. He resolved to assassinate his brother when returning form the Scottish wars, carry off the Lady, and make himself master of her person by force. – This scheme he imparted to me: he flattered, threatened, promised, and I yielded to his seduction!

ANG: Wretched man!

KENR: Condemn me not unheard. 'Tis true, that I followed Osmond to the scene of slaughter, but no blood that day imbrued my hand. It was the Earl whose sword struck Reginald to the ground: it was the Earl whose dagger was raised to complete his crime, when Evelina threw herself upon her husband's body, and received the weapon in her own.

ANG: Dreadful! Dreadful!

KENR: His hopes disappointed by this accident, Osmond's wrath became madness. He gave the word for slaughter, and Reginald's few attendants were butchered on the spot. Scarce could my prayers and arguments save from his wrath his infant niece, whose throat was already gored by his poniard. Angela, yours still wears that mark.

ANG: Mine? – Almighty powers!

KENR: Lady, 'tis true. I concealed in Allan's cottage the heiress of Conway: There were you doomed to languish in obscurity, till, alarmed by the report of his spies that Percy loved you, and dreading your meeting with so powerful a supporter, Osmond decreed your death a second time. With this intention he sought your retreat; but when in you he beheld Evelina's living image, he changed his bloody purpose. He caused me to reclaim you from Allan, and resolved, by making you his wife, to give himself a lawful claim to these possessions.

ANG: The monster! Now then I know, when he pressed my hand, why still my blood ran cold! 'Twas nature, that revolted at the fratricide's touch: 'Twas my mother's spirit, that whispered, 'Love not my murderer!' Oh! Good good Kenric! And you knelt to me for pardon? You, to whom I owe my life! You, to whom–

KENR: Hold! oh! hold! – Lady, how little do I deserve your thanks! – Oh! listen! listen!' – I was the last to quit the bloody spot: Sadly was I retiring, when a faint groan struck my ear. I sprang from my horse; I placed my hand on Reginald's heart; it beat beneath the pressure!

(Here Osmond appears at the door, motions to Saib, &c. to retire, and advances himself unobserved.)

ANG: It beat! It beat! Cruel, and your dagger–

KENR: Oh! that would have been mercy! No, Lady, I preserved his life to rob him of liberty. It struck me, how strong would be my hold over Osmond, while his brother was in my power; and this reflection determined me to preserve him. Having plunged the other bodies in the Conway's flood, I placed the bleeding Earl's on my horse before me, and conveyed him still insensible to a retreat, to all except myself a secret. There I tended his wounds carefully, and succeeded in preserving his life. – Lady, Reginald still exists.–

(Here Osmond with a furious look draws his dagger, and motions to stab Kenric. A moment's reflection makes him stay his hand, and he returns the weapon into the sheath.)

ANG: Still exists, say you? My father still exists?

KENR: He does, if a life so wretched can be termed existence. While his swoon lasted, I chained him to his dungeon wall; and no sooner were his wounds healed, than I entered his prison no more. Through a wicket in his dungeon-door I supplied him with food; and when in plaintive terms he sued to me for mercy, hasty I fled, nor gave an answer. Lady, near sixteen years have passed, since an human voice struck the ear of Reginald!

ANG: Alas! alas!

KENR: But the hour of his release draws near: I discovered this night that Osmond seeks my life, and resolved to throw myself on your mercy. Then tell me, Lady, will you plead for me with your father? Think you, he can forgive the author of his sufferings?

ANG: Kenric, you have been guilty, cruel – But restore to me my father; aid us to escape; and all shall be forgiven, all forgot.

KENR: Then follow me in silence: I will guide you to Reginald's dungeon: This key unlocks the Castle gates; and ere the cock crows, safe in the arms of Percy – (Here his eye falls upon Osmond, who has advanced between him and Angela. She shrieks, and sinks into a chair.)

Horror! – The Earl! – Undone for ever!

OSM: Miscreant! – Within there!

Enter Saib, Hassan, Muley, and Alaric.

OSM: Hence with that traitor! confine him in the western tower!

ANG: (Starting wildly from her seat.) Yet speak once more, Kenric! Where is my Father? What place conceals him?

OSM: Let him not speak! Away with him!

(Kenric is forced off by the Africans.)

OSM: (Paces the stage with a furious air, while Angela eyes him with terror: at length he stops, and addresses her.) Nay, stifle not your curses! Why should your lips be silent when your eye speaks? – Is there not written on every feature 'Vengeance on the assassin! Justice on my mother's murderer?' – But mark me, Angela! Compared to that which soon must be thine, these titles are sweet and lovely. Know'st thou the word parricide, Angela? Know'st thou their pangs who shed the blood of a parent? – Those pangs must be thine tomorrow. This long-concealed captive, this newfound father–

ANG: Your brother, Osmond? Your brother? – Surely you cannot, will not–

OSM: Still doubt you, that I both can, and will? – Remember Kenric's tale! Remember, though the first blow failed, the second will strike deeper! – But from whom must Reginald receive that second? Not from his rival brother! not from his inveterate foe! – From his daughter, his unfeeling daughter! 'Tis she, who, refusing me her hand, will place a dagger in mine; 'tis she, whose voice declaring that she hates me, will bid me plunge that dagger in her father's heart!

ANG: Man! man! drive me not mad!

OSM: (Pointing to Reginald's portrait.) Look upon this picture! Mark, what a noble form! How sweet, how commanding the expression of his full dark eye! – Then fancy that he lies in some damp solitary dungeon, writhing in death's agonies, his limbs distorted, his eye-strings breaking, his soul burthened with crimes from which no priest has absolved him, his last words curses on his unnatural child, who could have saved him, but who would not!

ANG: Horrible! horrible!

OSM: Yet if you still reject my offers, thus must it be. Tortures shall compel Kenric to reveal what dungeon conceals your father; and ere tomorrow dawns shall Angela lie a bride in my arms, or Reginald a corse at my feet. Nay, spare entreaties! Why should I heed your sorrows? You have gazed unmoved upon mine! Why should I be softened by your tears? Mine never were dried by your pity! Cold and inflexible have you been to my despair, so will I be to yours. Speak then, is Percy's love or your father's life most dear to you? Does the false mistress or the unnatural child sound most grating in your ears! Must Reginald die, or will Angela be mine?

ANG: Thine? – She will perish first!

OSM: You have pronounced his sentence, and his blood be on your head! – Farewell!

ANG: (Detaining him, and throwing herself on her knees.) Hold! hold! – Oh! – go not, go not yet! – Wretch that I am, where shall I fly for succour? – Mercy, Osmond! Oh! mercy, mercy! – Behold me at your feet, see me bathe them with my tears! Look with pity on a creature whom your cruelty has bowed to the earth, whose heart you have almost broken, whose brain you have almost turned! – Mercy, Osmond! – Oh! mercy! mercy!

OSM: Lovely, lovely suppliant! And why not profit by the present moment? Why owe to cold consent what force may this instant give me? – It shall be so, and thus – (Attempting to clasp her in his arms, she starts from the ground suddenly, and draws her dagger with a distracted look.)

ANG: Away! – Approach me not! – Dare not to touch me, or this poniard–

OSM: Foolish girl! Let me but say the word, and thou art disarmed that moment.

ANG: But not by thee, Osmond! Oh! never by thee! Hadst thou the force of fabled giants, vainly wouldst thou strive to wrest this dagger from my hand.

OSM: Let this convince you how easily – (Attempting to seize it, his eye rests upon the hilt, and he starts back with horror.) By hell, the very poniard which–

ANG: (In an exulting tone.) Ha! hast thou found me, villain? – Villain, dost thou know this weapon? Know'st thou whose blood incrusts the point? Murderer, it flowed from the bosom of my mother!

OSM: Within there! Help! (Hassan and Alaric enter.) Oh! God in heaven! (He falls senseless into their arms, and they convey him from the chamber: the door is locked after them.)

ANG: (Alone.) He faints! – Long may the villain wear thy chains, Oblivion! Long be it ere he wakes to commit new crimes! My father in Osmond's power? – Oh! 'tis a dreadful thought! – But no, it must not, shall not be! – I will to Osmond, will promise to be his, will sacrifice my love, my happiness, my peace of mind – every thing but my father! – Yet, to bid an assassin to rest upon my bosom, to press that hand in mine which pierced the heart of my parent – Oh! it were monstrous! – (Kneeling before Evelina's portrait.) Mother! Blessed Mother! If indeed thy spirit still lingers amidst these scenes of sorrow, look on my despair with pity! fly to my aid! oh! fly, and save my father! – (She remains for some moments prostrate on the ground in silent sorrow. The Castle-bell tolls the hour: she raises herself and counts the quarters, after which it strikes 'one!') Hark! the bell tolls! – 'Tis the time which the Monk appointed. He will not tarry: But I must not follow him; I will not fly and abandon my father! – Yet may not my flight preserve him? Yes, yes, I will away to Percy: By the same passage which favours my escape, his vassals may easily surprise the Castle, may seize Osmond ere he effects his crime, and tomorrow may see Reginald restored to freedom, to his domains, and to his daughter! – Oh! then sweet indeed will be my feelings! Then only can my heart know joy, when it throbs against a father's! – Ha! what was that! Methought the sound of music floated by me! It seemed as some one had struck the guitar! – I must have been deceived; it was but fancy.

(A plaintive voice sings within, accompanied by a guitar.)

'Lullaby! – Lullaby! – Hush thee, my dear,

Thy father is coming, and soon will be here!'

ANG: Heavens! The very words which Alice – The door too! – It moves! it opens! – Guard me, good Angels!

(The folding-doors unclose, and the Oratory is seen illuminated. In its centre stands a tall female figure, her white and flowing garments spotted with blood; her veil is thrown back, and discovers a pale and melancholy countenance; her eyes are lifted upwards, her arms extended towards heaven, and a large wound appears upon her bosom. Angela sinks upon her knees, with her eyes riveted upon the figure, which for some moments remains motionless. At length the Spectre advances slowly, to a soft and plaintive strain; she stops opposite to Reginald's picture, and gazes upon it in silence. She then turns, approaches Angela, seems to invoke a blessing upon her, points to the picture, and retires to the Oratory. The music ceases. Angela rises with a wild look, and follows the Vision, extending her arms towards it.)

ANG: Stay, lovely spirit! – Oh! stay yet one moment!

(The Spectre waves her hand, as bidding her farewell. Instantly the organ's swell is heard; a full chorus of female voices chaunt 'Jubilate!' a blaze of light flashes through the Oratory, and the folding doors close with a loud noise.)

ANG: Oh! Heaven protect me! – (She falls motionless on the floor.)

END OF THE FOURTH ACT

ACT V

SCENE I. – A View of Conway Castle by moonlight.

Enter Percy and Motley.

MOTL: In truth, my Lord, you venture too near the Castle. Should you fall into Osmond's power a second time, your next jump may be into a better world.

PERCY: Oh! there is no danger, Motley. My followers are not far off, and will join me at a moment's warning; then fear not for me.

MOTL: With all my heart, but permit me to fear for myself. We are now within bowshot of the Castle. The archers may think proper to amuse us with a proof of their skill; and were I to feel an arrow quivering in my gizzard, probably I should be much more surprised than pleased. Good my Lord, let us back to the fisherman's hut.

PERCY: Your advice may be wise, Gilbert, but I cannot follow it. Angela's escape may be discovered: she may be pursued, and in need of my assistance. Then counsel not my retiring; my fears of losing Angela are too strong, the flame which burns in my bosom too ardent!

MOTL: I'm sure no flame burning in your bosom can give you so much pain as an arrow would give me sticking in mine; and as to your fears of losing the Lady, I'd bet mine of losing my life against any fears in Christendom!

PERCY: How, Gilbert? Have you not promised to stand by me to the last? Did you not say you could die in my service with pleasure?

MOTL: Very true. – But, Lord! if a man was always taken at his word, the world would soon be turned upside down. When a polite gentleman begs you to consider his house as your own, and assures you that all he has is at your disposal, he'd be in a terrible scrape if you began knocking down his walls, or requested the loan of his wife or daughters! – No, no, Sir! When I said that I should die in your service with pleasure, I intended to live in it many long years; since, to tell you the truth, from a child I had always a particular dislike to dying, and I think that with every hour the prejudice grows stronger. – Good my Lord, let us begone. Ere long I doubt not–

PERCY: Hark! Did I not hear – No! She comes not! – Heavens, should the Friar's plot have failed!

MOTL: Failed, and a Priest and a Petticoat concerned in it? – Oh! no; a plot composed of such good ingredients cannot but succeed. – Ugh! Would I were again seated by the Fisher's hearth! The wind blows cruel sharp and bitter!

PERCY: For shame, Gilbert! Am I not equally exposed to its severity?

MOTL: Oh! The flame in your bosom keeps you warm; and in a cold night love wraps one up better than a blanket.[9] But that not being my situation, the present

---

[9] Sancho makes nearly the same observation upon sleep.

object of my desires is a blazing wood-fire, and Venus would look to me less lovely than a smoking sack posset! – Oh! when I was in love, I managed matters much better: I always paid my addresses by the fireside, and contrived to urge my soft suit just at dinnertime. Then how I filled my fair-one's ears with fine speeches, while she filled my trencher with roast-beef! Then what figures and tropes came out of my mouth, and what dainties and tidbits went in! 'Twould have done your heart good to hear me talk, and see me eat and you'd have found it no easy matter to decide, whether I had most wit or appetite.

PERCY: And who was the object of this voracious passion?

MOTL: A person well calculated to charm both my heart and my stomach: It was a Lady of great merit, who did your Father the honour to superintend his culinary concerns. I was scarce fifteen, when she kindled a flame in my heart, while lighting the kitchen fire, and from that moment I thought on nothing but her. My mornings were passed in composing poems on her beauty, my evenings in reciting them in her ear; for Nature had equally denied the fair creature and myself the faculty of reading and writing.

PERCY: You were successful, I hope?

MOTL: Why, at length, my Lord, a Pindaric Ode upon her grace in frying pancakes melted her heart. She consented to be mine; when, oh! cruel Fortune! taking one night a drop too much – poor dear creature! she never got the better of it! I wept her loss, and composed an Elegy upon it, which has been thought, by many persons of great judgment, not totally destitute of taste and sublimity. It began thus:

Baked be the pies to coals! Burn, roast-meat, burn!

Boil o'er, ye pots! Ye spits, forget to turn!

Cindrelia's death—

PERCY: Peace! peace! – See you nothing near yonder tower?

MOTL: Yes, certainly. Two persons advance towards us: Yet they cannot be our friends, for I see neither the Lady's petticoat nor the Monk's paunch!

PERCY: Still they approach, though slowly: One leans on his companion, and seems to move with pain. Let us retire and observe them.

MOTL: Away, Sir: I'm at your heels.

(They draw back.)

(Enter Saib conducting Kenric.)

SAIB: Nay, yet hold up a while! – Now we are near the Fisher's cottage.

KENR: Good Saib, I needs must stop! – Enfeebled by Osmond's tortures, my limbs refuse to bear me further! – Here lay me down: Then fly to Percy, guide him to the dungeon, and, ere 'tis too late, bid him save the Father of Angela!

PERCY: (To Motley.) – Hark! Did you hear?

SAIB: Yet, to leave you thus alone!–

KENR: Oh! Heed not me! Think, that on these few moments depends our safety, Angela's freedom, Reginald's life! – You have the master-key! Fly then – oh! fly to Percy!

PERCY (Starting forward.) – Said he not Reginald? – Speak again, stranger! What of Reginald?

SAIB: Ha! Look up, Kenric! – 'Tis Percy's-self!

PERCY AND MOTLEY. How! – Kenric?

KENR: (Sinking at Percy's feet.) Yes, the guilty, the penitent Kenric! Oh! surely 'twas Heaven sent you hither! Know, Earl Percy, that Reginald lives, that Angela is his daughter!

PERCY: Amazement! – And is this known to Osmond?

KENR: Two hours have scarcely passed since he surprised the secret. Tortures compelled me to avow where Reginald was hidden, and he now is in his brother's power. Fly then to his aid! Alas! perhaps at this moment his destruction is completed! Perhaps even now Osmond's dagger–

PERCY: Within there! Allan! Harold! – Quick, Gilbert, sound your horn! – (Motley sounds it.)

(Enter Allan, Edric, Harold, and Soldiers.)

PERCY: Friends, may I depend on your support?

HAR. While we breathe, all will stand by you!

SOLDIERS. All! – All!

PERCY: Follow me then! – Away!

KENR: Yet stay one moment! – Percy, to this grateful friend have I confided a master-key, which will instantly admit you to the Castle, and have described to him the retreat of Reginald! – Be he your guide, and hasten – Oh! that pang! – (He faints; Allan and Edric support him.)

PERCY: Look to him! He sinks! Bear him to your hut, Edric, and there tend his hurts – (To Saib.) Now on, good fellow, and swiftly! – Osmond, despair, I come!

(Exit with Saib, Motley, Harold, and Soldiers on one side, while Allan and Edric convey away Kenric still fainting on the other.)

***

SCENE II. – A Vaulted Chamber.

Enter Father Philip, with a Basket on his Arm and a Torch, conducting Angela.

F. PHIL: Thanks to St. Francis, we have as yet passed unobserved! – Surely, of all travelling companions, Fear is the least agreeable: I couldn't be more fatigued, had I run twenty miles without stopping!

ANG: Why this delay? – Good Father, let us proceed.

F. PHIL: Ere I can go further, Lady, I must needs stop to take breath, and refresh my spirits with a taste of this cordial – (Taking a bottle from the basket.)

ANG: Oh! Not now! Think that Osmond may discover me, and mar your kind intentions. This room, you say, conceals the private door: Pr'ythee, unclose it! Let us from hence! Wait till we are safe under Percy's protection, and then drink as you list. But not now, Father; in pity, not now!

F. PHIL: Well, well, be calm, Daughter! – Oh! these women! these women! They mind no one's comfort but their own! – Now, where is the door?

ANG: How tedious seems every moment which I pass within these hated walls! – Ha! Yonder comes a light!

F. PHIL: So, so – I've found it at last – (Touching a spring, a secret door flies open.)

ANG: It moves this way! – By all my fears, 'tis Osmond! – In, Father, in! – Away, for Heaven's sake! (Exeunt, closing the door after them)

(Enter Osmond and Hassan with a Torch.)

OSM: (After a pause of gloomy meditation.) Is all still within the Castle?

HASS: As the silence of the grave.

OSM: Where are your fellows?

HASS: Saib guards the traitor Kenric: Muley and Alaric are buried in sleep.

OSM: Their hands have been stained in blood, and yet can they sleep? – Call your companions hither. – (Hassan offers to leave the torch.) – Away with the light! Its beams are hateful!

(Exit Hassan)

OSM: (Alone.) Yes! this is the place. If Kenric said true, for sixteen years have the vaults beneath me rang with my brother's groans. I dread to unclose the door! How shall I sustain the beams of his eye when they rest on Evelina's murderer? How will his proud heart swell with rage at meeting his usurping brother! – Ah! the beams of his eye must long since have been quenched in tears! – The pride of his heart must by this be subdued by suffering! – Great have been those sufferings – in truth so great, that even my hatred bends before them. – Yet for that hatred had I not cause? At Tournaments, 'twas to Reginald that each noble proffered friendship. Evelina too! – Ha! at that name my expiring hate revives! Reginald! Reginald! For thee was I sacrificed! Oh! When it strikes a second blow, my poniard shall stab surer!

Enter Hassan, Muley, and Alaric, with Torches

THE AFRICANS. (Together.) My Lord! My Lord!

OSM: Now, why this haste?

HASS: I tremble to inform you, that Saib has fled the Castle. A master-key, which he found upon Kenric, and of which he kept possession, has enabled him to escape.

OSM: Saib too gone? – All are false! All forsake me!

HASS: Yet more, my Lord; he has made his prisoner the companion of his flight.

OSM: (Starting.) How? Kenric escaped?

ALARIC. 'Tis but too certain; doubtless he has fled to Percy.

OSM: To Percy! – Ha! Then I must be speedy: my fate hangs on a thread! Friends, I have ever found ye faithful; mark me now! – (Opening the private door.) Of these two passages, the left conducts to a long chain of dungeons: In one of these my brother still languishes. Once already have you seen him bleeding beneath my sword – but he yet exists. My fortune, my love, nay my life, are at stake! Need I say more? (Each half-unsheathes his sword.) – That gesture speaks me understood. On then before, I follow you. (The Africans pass through the private door: Osmond is advancing toward it, when he suddenly starts back.) – Ha! Why roll these seas of blood before me? Whose mangled corse do they bear to my feet? – Fratricide? – Oh! 'tis a dreadful name! – Yet how preserve myself and Reginald? – It cannot be! We must not breathe the same atmosphere. – Fate, thy hand urges me! – Fate, thy voice prompts me! Thou hast spoken; I obey. – (He follows the Africans; the door is closed after them.)

***

SCENE III. – A gloomy subterraneous Dungeon, wide and lofty: The upper part of it has in several places fallen in, and left large chasms. On one side are various passages leading to other Caverns: On the other is an Iron Door with steps leading to it, and a Wicket in the middle. Reginald, pale and emaciated, in coarse garments, his hair hanging wildly about his face, and a chain bound round his body, lies sleeping upon a bed of straw. A lamp, a small basket, and a pitcher, are placed near him. After a few moments he awakes, and extends his arms.

REG: My child! My Evelina! – Oh! fly me not, lovely forms! – They are gone, and once more I live to misery. – Thou wert kind to me, Sleep! Even now, methought, I sat in my Castle-hall: A maid, lovely as the Queen of Fairies, hung on my knee, and hailed me by that sweet name, 'Father!' Yes, I was happy! – Yet frown not on me therefore, Darkness! I am thine again, my gloomy bride! – Be not incensed, Despair, that I left thee for a moment; I have passed with thee sixteen years! Ah! how many have I still to pass? – Yet fly not my bosom quite, sweet Hope! Still speak to me of liberty, of light! Whisper, that once more I shall see the morn break, that again shall my fevered lips drink the pure gale of evening! – God, thou know'st that I have borne my sufferings meekly; I have wept for myself, but never cursed my foes; I have sorrowed for thy anger, but never murmured at thy will. Patient have I been; oh! then reward me! let me once again press my daughter in my arms; let me, for one instant, feel again that I clasp to my heart a being who loves me! Speed thou to heaven, prayer of a captive! – (*He sinks upon a stone, with his* hands clasped, and his eyes bent stedfastly upon the flame of the lamp.)

(Angela and Father Philip are seen through the chasms above, passing along slowly.)

ANG: Be cautious, Father! – Feel you not how the ground trembles beneath us?

F. PHIL: Perfectly well; and would give my best breviary to find myself once more on terra-firma. But the outlet cannot be far off: Let us proceed.

ANG: Look down upon us, blessed Angels! Aid us! protect us!

F. PHIL: Amen, fair daughter! – And now away. (Exeunt.)

REG: (After a pause.) 'Tis that door which divides me from happiness. How often against that door have I knelt and prayed, and ever knelt and prayed in vain! Fearful, lest my complaints should move him from his purpose, my gaoler listens not, replies not: Hasty through yon wicket he gives my food, then flies as if this dungeon held a serpent. Oh! then how my heart swells with bitterness, when the sound of his retiring steps is heard no more, when through yon lofty chasm I catch no longer the gleam of his departing torch! – How wastes my lamp? The hour of Kenric's visit must long be past, and still he comes not. How, if death's hand hath struck him suddenly? My existence unknown – Away from my fancy, dreadful idea! (Rising, and taking the lamp.) The breaking of my chain permits me to wander at large through the wide precincts of my prison. Haply the late storm, whose pealing thunders were heard e'en in this abyss, may have rent some friendly chasm: Haply some nook yet unexplored – Ah! no, no, no! My hopes are vain, my search will be fruitless. Despair in these dungeons reigns despotic; she mocks my complaints, rejects my prayers, and, when I sue for freedom, bids me seek it in my grave! – Death! Oh! Death! how welcome wilt thou be to me!

(Exit)

(The noise is heard of an heavy bar falling; the door opens.)

(Enter Father Philip and Angela.)

F. PHIL: How's this? A door?

ANG: It was barred on the outside.

F. PHIL: That we'll forgive, as it wasn't bolted on the in. But I don't recollect – Surely I've not–

ANG: What's the matter?

F. PHIL: By my faith, daughter, I suspect that I've missed my way.

ANG: Heaven forbid!

F. PHIL: Nay, if 'tis so, I sha'n't be the first man who of two ways has preferred the wrong.

ANG: Provoking! And did I not tell you to chuse the right-hand passage?

F. PHIL: Truly, did you; and that was the very thing which made me chuse the left. Whenever I'm in doubt myself, I generally ask a woman's advice. When she's of one way of thinking, I've always found that reason's on the other. In this instance, perhaps, I have been mistaken: But wait here for one moment, and the fact shall be ascertained. But, perhaps, you fear being alone in the dark?

ANG: I fear nothing, except Osmond.

F. PHIL: Nay, I've no more inclination to fall into his clutches again, than yourself. What would be the consequence? You would be married, I should be hung! Now, daughter, you may think that I've a very bad taste; but as, I'm a Christian, I'd rather be married fifty years, than hung for one little half-hour. (Exit)

ANG: How thick and infectious is the air of this cavern! Yet perhaps for sixteen years has my poor father breathed none purer. Hark! Steps are quick advancing! The Friar comes, but why in such confusion?

(Re-enter Father Philip running.)

F. PHIL: Help! Help! It follows me!

ANG: (Detaining him.) What alarms you? Speak!

F. PHIL: His ghost! his ghost! – Let me go! – let me go! – let me go! (Struggling to escape from Angela, he falls, and extinguishes the torch; then hastily rises, and rushes up the staircase, throwing the door after him.)

ANG: (Alone.) Father! Father! Stay, for heaven's sake! – He's gone, I cannot find the door! Hark! – 'Twas the clank of chains! – A light too! It comes yet nearer! – Save me, ye powers! – What dreadful form! 'Tis here! I faint with terror! – (Sinks almost lifeless against the dungeon's side.)

Re-enter Reginald with a lamp.

REG: He is gone! – Emaciated and stiff from long disuse, scarce can I draw my limbs along, and I strive in vain to overtake the fugitive.

ANG: (Recovering herself.) Still is it there, that fearful vision!

REG: (Placing his lamp upon a pile of stones.) Why did Kenric enter my prison? Haply, when he heard not my groans at the dungeon door, he thought that my woes were relieved by death. Oh! when will that thought be verified?

ANG: How sunk his eye! – How wildly hangs his matted hair on his pale and furrowed brow! – Oh! those are the furrows of anguish, not of age.

REG: I have oft wiped away tears, but never caused them to flow; oft have I lightened the prisoner's chains, but never increased their burthen: Yet I am doomed to chains and tears!

ANG: Each sound of his hollow plaintive voice strikes to my heart. Dared I accost him – Yet perhaps a maniac – No matter; he suffers, and the accents of pity will flow sweetly in his ears!

REG: Thou art dead, and at rest, my wife! Safe in yon skies, no thought of me molests thy quiet. Yet sure I wrong thee! At the hour of death thy spirit shall stand beside me, shall close mine eyes gently, and murmur, 'Die, Reginald, and be at peace!'

ANG: Hark! Heard I not – Pardon, good stranger–

REG: (Starting wildly from his seat.) 'Tis she! She comes for me! Is the hour at hand, fair vision? Spirit of Evelina, lead on, I follow thee! (He extends his arms toward her, staggers a few paces forwards, then sinks exhausted on the ground.)

ANG: He faints! perhaps expires! – Still, still! See, he revives!

REG: 'Tis gone! Once more the sport of my bewildered brain – (Starting up.) Powers of bliss! Look, where it moves again! – Oh! say, what art thou? If Evelina, speak, oh! speak!

ANG: Ha! Named he not Evelina? That look! – This dungeon too! – The emotions which his voice – It is, it must be! – Father! Oh! Father! Father! – (Falling upon his bosom.)

REG: Said you? – Meant you? – My daughter – my infant, whom I left – Oh! yes, it must be true! My heart, which springs towards you, acknowledges my child! – (Embracing her.)

ANG: And is it thus I find you? Burthened with chains, no warmth, no air, no comfort!

REG: Think of it no more, my dearest! But say, how gained you entrance? Has Osmond–

ANG: Oh! that name recalls my terrors! – Alas! you see in me a fugitive from his violence! Guided by a friendly Monk, whom your approach has frightened from me, I was endeavouring to escape: We missed our way, and chance guided us to this dungeon. But this is not a time for explanation. Answer me! Know you the subterraneous passages belonging to this Castle?

REG: Whose entrance is without the walls? I do.

ANG: Then we may yet be saved! Father, we must fly this moment. Percy, the pride of our English youth, waits for me at the Conway's side. Come then, oh! come! Stay not one moment longer. (As she approaches the door, lights appear above.)

REG: Look! look, my child! The beams of distant torches flash through the gloom!

ANG: Ha! – Yet, perhaps, ashamed of his desertion, 'tis but the Monk, who returns to seek me.

REG: Grant, Heaven, that it may prove so!

OSM: (Above.) Hassan, guard you the door. – Follow me, friends–

The lights disappear.

ANG: Osmond's voice? Undone! Undone! Oh! my father! he comes to seek you, perhaps to – Oh! 'tis a word too dreadful for a daughter's lips!

REG: If he seeks none but me, I am happy: But should your steps have been traced, my child – Hark! they come! The gloom of yonder cavern may awhile conceal you: Fly to it: Hide yourself: Stir not, I charge you.

ANG: What, leave you? Oh! no, no!

REG: Dearest, I entreat, I conjure you, fly! Fear not for me! – Hark! they are at the door! Speed to the cavern! Speak not, move not; if possible, breathe not!

ANG: Father! Oh! Father!

REG: Farewel! perhaps for ever! – (He forces Angela into the cavern, then returns hastily, and throws himself on the bed of straw.) – Now then to hear my doom!

(Enter Osmond, followed by Muley and Alaric with torches.)

OSM: The door unbarred? – Softly, my fears were false! – Lo! where stretched on the ground, straw his couch, a stone his pillow, he tastes that repose which flies from my bed of down! – Wake, Reginald, and arise!

REG: You here, Osmond? What brings you to this scene of sorrow? Alas! hope flies while I gaze upon your frowning eye! Have I read its language aright, Osmond?

OSM: Aright, if you have read my hatred. Reginald, I bring you death! – What other present could you expect from me? Have you not been ever a thorn in my path, a speck in my sight? Was not 'Submit to your elder brother,' the galling lesson for ever sounded in my ears? And when I praised some favourite spot of these domains, some highbrowed hill, or blooming valley, was not my father's answer still, 'That will be your elder brother's?' Yes, the first thought which struck my brain was, 'I am a younger son!' The first passion which tortured my heart was hate to him that made me one!

REG: Have I deserved that hate? You often injured me, but as often I forgave. You were ever my foe, but I never forgot you were my brother.

OSM: Hypocrite!

REG: Was I one when my weapon struck the fierce Scot to the ground, whose sword already glittered above your head? Was I one when, as embarrassed by your armour you sank beneath the Severn's waves, I sprang into the flood, I seized, I saved you? Twice have I preserved your life! Oh! let it not be for my own destruction! See, my brother, the once proud Reginald lies at your feet, for his pride has been humbled by suffering! Hear him adjure you by her ashes, within whose bosom we both have lain, not to stain your hands with the blood of your brother!

OSM: (Aside.) He melts me in my own despite!

REG: The fountains of my eyes have been long dried up: I have no tears that can soften, no eloquence that can persuade; but Heaven has lightnings that can blast! Then, spare me, Osmond! Kenric has told me that my daughter lives! Restore me to her arms; permit us in obscurity to pass our days together! Then shall my last sigh implore upon your head Heaven's forgiveness, and Evelina's.

OSM: It shall be so. – Rise, Reginald, and hear me! You mentioned even now your daughter: Know, she is in my power; know also, that I love her!

REG: How?

OSM: She rejects my offers. Your authority can oblige her to accept them. Swear to use it, and this instant will I lead you to her arms.

REG: Osmond, she is your niece!

OSM: I have influence at Rome – That obstacle will be none to me. – What is your answer! You hesitate! Say, will you give the demanded oath?

REG: I cannot dissemble; Osmond, I never will.[10]

OSM: How? – Reflect that your life–

REG: Would be valueless, if purchased by my daughter's tears; would be loathsome, if embittered by my daughter's misery. Osmond I will not take the oath.

OSM: (Almost choked with passion.) – 'Tis enough! – (To the Africans.) – You know your duty! Drag him to yonder cavern! Let me not see him die!

REG: (Holding by a fragment of the wall, from which the Africans strive to force him.) – Brother, for pity's sake! for your soul's happiness!

---

[10] This is the third time that Osmond has asked the same question, and the poor man always receives the same answer.

OSM: Obey me, slaves! – Away!

Angela rushes in wildly.

ANG: Hold off! – Hurt him not! He is my father!

OSM: Angela here?

REG: Daughter, what means–

ANG: (Embracing him.) – You shall live, Father! I will sacrifice all to preserve you! – Here is my hand, Osmond! 'Tis yours; but spare my father!

OSM: (Transported.) – Lovely Angela!–

REG: How, rash girl! What would you do?

OSM: Reginald, reflect–

REG: Your uncle! Your mother's murderer! – Remember–

ANG: Your life is in danger; I must forget all else. – Osmond, release my father, and solemnly I swear–

REG: Hold, girl, and first hear me! – (Kneeling.) – God of Nature, to Thee I call! – If e'er on Osmond's bosom a child of mine rests; if e'er she calls him husband who pierced her hapless mother's heart, that moment shall a wound, by my own hand inflicted–

ANG: Hold! – Oh! hold! – End not your oath!

OSM: I burn with rage!

REG: Swear never to be Osmond's!

ANG: I swear!—

REG: Be repaid by this embrace!

OSM: Be it your last! — Tear them asunder!

ANG: Away! Away! I will not leave him.

OSM: Part them, I say! — Ha! what noise?

Enter Hassan, hastily.

HASS: My Lord, all is lost! — Percy has stormed the Castle, and speeds this way!

OSM: Confusion! — Then I must be sudden. Aid me, Hassan! (Hassan and Osmond force Angela from her Father, who suddenly disengages himself from Muley and Alaric.)

REG: Friends so near? — Villains! at least you shall buy my life dearly! — (Suddenly seizing Hassan's sword.)

OSM: (Employed with Hassan in retaining Angela, while Reginald defends himself against Muley and Alaric.) — Down with him! — Wrest the sword from him! — (Alaric is wounded, and falls; Muley gives back; at the same time, Osmond's party appears above, pursued by Percy's.) — Hark! They come! — Dastardly villains! — Nay, then, my own hand must — (Drawing his sword, he rushes upon Reginald, who is disarmed, and beaten upon his knees; when at the moment that Osmond lifts his arm to stab him, Evelina's Ghost throws herself between them: Osmond starts back, and drops his sword.)

OSM: Horror! – What form is this?

ANG: Die! (Disengaging herself from Hassan, she springs suddenly forwards, and plunges her dagger into Osmond's bosom, who falls with a loud groan, and faints. The Ghost vanishes; Angela and Reginald rush into each other's arms.)

ANG: Father, thou art mine again!

(Enter Percy, Motley, Saib, Harold, &c. pursuing Osmond's party. All stop on seeing him bleeding upon the ground.)

PERCY: Hold, my brave friends! – See where lies the object of our search!

ANG: Percy! – Dear Percy!

PERCY: (Flying to her.) – Dearest Angela!

ANG: My friend, my guardian angel! Come, Percy, come! embrace my father! – Father, embrace the protector of your child!

PERCY: Do I then behold Earl Reginald?

REG: (Embracing him.) – The same, brave Percy! Welcome to my heart! Live ever next it!

ANG: Oh, moment that o'erpays my sufferings! – And yet – Percy, that wretched man – He perished by my hand!

SAIB: Hark, he sighs! – There is life still in him!

ANG: Life? – Then save him, save him! Bear him to his chamber! Look to his wound! Heal it, if possible! At least gain him time to repent his crime and errors! – (Osmond is conveyed away:– Servants enter with torches, and the Stage becomes light.)

PERCY: Though ill-deserved by his guilt, your generous pity still is amiable. But say, fair Angela, what have I to hope? Is my love approved by your noble father? Will he–

REG: Percy, this is no time to talk of love. Let me hasten to my expiring brother, and soften with forgiveness the pangs of death!

PERCY: And can you forget your sufferings?

REG: Ah! youth, has he had none? Oh! in his stately chambers, far greater must have been his pangs than mine in this gloomy dungeon; for what gave me comfort was his terror, what gave me hope was his despair. I knew that I was guiltless; knew that, though I suffered in this world, my lot would be happy in that to come!

> And, Oh thou wretch! whom hopeless woes oppress,
> Whose day no joys, whose night no slumbers bless!
> When pale Despair alarms thy phrensied eye,
> Screams in thine ear, and bids thee Heaven deny,
> Court thou Religion! Strive thy faith to save;
> Bend thy fixed glance on bliss beyond the grave;
> Hush guilty murmurs; banish dark mistrust;
> Think there's a Power above, nor doubt that Power is just!

FINIS.

EPILOGUE

Spoken by Mrs. Jordan.

Osmond by this arrived at Charon's ferry,
My honour saved, and dad alive and merry,
Hither I come the public doom to know,
But come not uncompell'd – the more's my woe!
E'en now, (oh! pity, friends, my hard mishap!)
My shoulder felt a Bow-Street runner's tap,
Who, while I shook with fear in every limb,
Thus spoke, with accent stern and visage grim–
'Mistress!' quoth he, 'to me it given in trust is,
'To bring you straight before our larned Justice;
'For, know, 'tis said, tonight, the whole town o'er,
'You've kill'd one Osmond, alias Barrymore.'
'The fellow's mad!' 'twas thus amaz'd I spoke;
'Lord! Sir, I murdered Osmond for a joke.
'This dagger, free from blood, will make it certain,
'He died but till the prompter dropped the curtain;
'And now, well pleased to quit this scene of riot,
'The man's gone home to sup in peace and quiet!'
Finding that all I said was said in vain,
And Townshend still his first design maintain,
I thought 'twere best to fly for shelter here,
And beg my generous friends to interfere.
But though the awkward nature of my case
May spread some slight confusion o'er my face,
No terrors awe my bosom, I'll assure ye;
Just is my cause, and English is my jury!
Besides, it must appear, on explanation,
How very ticklish was my situation,
And all perforce, his crimes when I relate,
Must own that Osmond well deserved his fate.

He heeded not papa's pathetic pleading;
He stabbed mama – which was extreme ill-breeding;
And at his feet for mercy when I sued,
The odious wretch, I vow, was downright rude.
Twice his bold hands my person dared to touch!
Twice in one day! – 'Twas really once too much!
And therefore justly filled with virtuous ire,
To save my honour, and protect my sire,
I drew my knife, and in his bosom stuck it;
He fell, you clapped – and then he kicked the bucket!
So perish still the wretch, whose soul can know
Selfish delight, while causing other's woe;
Who blasts that joy, the sweetest God has given,
And makes an hell, where love would make an heaven!
Forbear, thou lawless libertine! nor seek
Forc'd favours on that pale averted cheek:
If thy warm kisses cost bright eyes one tear,
Kisses from loveliest lips are bought too dear–
Unless those lips with thine keep playful measure,
And that sweet tear should be a tear of pleasure!
Now as for Osmond – at that villain's name
I feel reviving wrath my soul inflame!
And shall one short and sudden pang suffice
To clear so base a fault, so gross a vice?
No! To your bar, dear friends, for aid I fly!
Bid Osmond live again, again to die;
Nightly with plaudits loud his breath recall,
Nightly beneath my dagger see him fall,
Give him a thousand lives! – and let me take them all.

www.ReadHowYouWant.com

You can buy our **Large Type** and **EasyRead** books from our www.ReadHowYouWant.com website, from websites like Amazon.com and through your UK and North American bookshop.

EasyRead books are designed to make your reading easy and enjoyable. **EasyRead** books are published in different font sizes, so you can select the font size best for you.

EasyRead is for people with normal eyesight who want books in an easy-to-read format.

EasyRead Comfort is for people who find reading small print tiring but do not need large print.

EasyRead Large is for people who find it easier to read larger print.

The **EasyRead** font, character, word and line spacing have all been set to make it as easy as possible both to recognize a word, and to run your eye along a line of text without losing your place. We split as few words as possible at line ends, as split words make reading harder and can be annoying. For out-of-copyright books, words have been changed to modern spelling (where the sense is not affected), and the original hyphenation of compound words has been retained where this improves word recognition or sense.

With most things you buy, you get a choice, and you can choose the make and model that suits best. There is a big exception – books. You don't get to choose a format that is easy for you to read – you have to read the format the publisher selects.

This **"One Size Fits All"** paradigm **no longer** need apply to books.

At www.ReadHowYouWant.com, you can order a book just as you want it, so you can read it easily. You can choose nearly any format, and at a surprisingly low cost, because of a technical breakthrough that allows us to typeset an individual book automatically, print and bind the book and have it quickly sent directly to you.

You can have your book in **Talking Book** formats (**DAISY or MP3**) or as an **E-book** or in **Braille**.

We have developed totally new visual formats which we hope will help people with **dyslexia** and other print reading disabilities. Look at www.ReadHowYouWant.com for more information.

Good news for publishers and authors. There is a big market for large type, personalized and accessible format books. We can help publishers and authors find new market opportunities for their books, and selling your book through www.ReadHowYouWant.com is easy – we do the work for you. Contact us on info@ReadHowYouWant.com.

Made in the USA
San Bernardino, CA
16 April 2015